Microwave Magic

Index

Grolier Limited

TORONTO

Contributors to this series:

Recipes and Technical Assistance:
École de cuisine Bachand-Bissonnette
Cooking consultants:
Denis Bissonette
Michèle Émond
Dietician:
Christiane Barbeau
Photos:
Laramée Morel Communications
Audio-Visuelles
Design:
Claudette Taillefer
Assistants:
Julie Deslauriers
Philippe O'Connor
Joan Pothier
Accessories:
Andrée Cournoyer
Writing:
Communications La Griffe Inc.
Text Consultants:
Cap et bc inc.
Advisors:
Roger Aubin
Joseph R. De Varennes
Gaston Lavoie
Kenneth H. Pearson

Assembly:
Carole Garon
Vital Lapalme
Jean-Pierre Larose
Carl Simmons
Gus Soriano
Marc Vallières
Production Managers:
Gilles Chamberland
Ernest Homewood
Production Assistants:
Martine Gingras
Catherine Gordon
Kathy Kishimoto
Peter Thomlison
Art Director:
Bernard Lamy
Editors:
Laurielle Ilacqua
Susan Marshall
Margaret Oliver
Robin Rivers
Lois Rock
Jocelyn Smyth
Donna Thomson
Dolores Williams
Development:
Le Groupe Polygone Éditeurs Inc.

We wish to thank the following firms, PIER I IMPORTS and LE CACHE POT, for their contribution to the illustration of this set.

Canadian Cataloguing in Publication Data

Main entry under title:

Index

(Microwave magic ; 26)
Index to v. 1-25 of Microwave magic.
Translation of: Index.
Includes index.
ISBN 0-7172-2447-3

1. Microwave magic (Toronto, Ont.)—Indexes.
2. Microwave cookery—Indexes.
I. Series: Microwave magic (Toronto, Ont.) ; 26.

TX832.I5313 1988   641.5'882   C88-094227-4

Contents

Note from the Editor................................. 6

Power Levels....................................... 7

Special Characteristics of the Microwave Oven........... 8

Microwave Cooking Accessories....................... 10

Utensils for Measurement and Preparation.............. 14

Utensils for Cooking and Reheating................... 18

Dishes for Cooking and Reheating.................... 20

Alphabetical Index................................. 25

Thematic Index.................................... 71

Microtips Index....................................101

Microwave Magic is a multi-volume set, with each volume devoted to a particular type of cooking. So, if you are looking for a chicken recipe, you simply go to one of the two volumes that deal with poultry. Each volume has its own index, and the final volume contains a general index to the complete set.

Microwave Magic puts over twelve hundred recipes at your fingertips. You will find it as useful as the microwave oven itself. Enjoy!

Note from the Editor

Finding the Information You Need

Microwave Magic, with its 25 volumes of recipes, constitutes a real mine of information on all aspects of the art of cooking as adapted to the technology of the microwave oven. In order to make the set as easy as possible for you to use, the contents of the volumes have been organized thematically. Thus, for example, if you wish to satisfy a craving for shrimps, you can turn directly to Volume 6 entitled *Seafood* and consult its index in order to find the recipe that best suits the mood of the moment. On the other hand, if you want to prepare something special but have no specific dish in mind, you might well wish to look over the entire range of possibilities without having to consult each of the 25 books in turn.

The purpose of this general Index to the set is to enable you to do just that. Actually, what we are presenting here is really three indexes in one.

To begin with, there is an Alphabetical index (pages 25 to 69) in which are listed all the recipes and all the articles found in the 25 volumes. This index will be particularly useful to you if you already know the name of the dish you wish to prepare or if you are looking for technical information (on cooking, on defrosting, etc). Longer than either of the other indexes, this one will probably be the one you find yourself using most.

We have also provided a Thematic index (pages 71 to 100) in which we have classified both recipes and information according to the various themes dealt with in the set. For example, under the heading **Beef** you will find a list of all the recipes using beef as their main ingredient. Practical and easy to use, the Thematic Index will quickly guide you to the recipe or recipes that can satisfy your immediate needs, whatever those may be.

Finally, we have also prepared an alphabetical index (pages 101 to 109) of the numerous MICROTIPS scattered through the 25 volumes of *Microwave Magic.* This list will direct you to a wealth of practical information that will help ensure the success of your efforts and at the same time enable you to add the personal and out-of-the-way touches that are the hallmark of an accomplished cook.

We feel certain that with the help of these three indices, you will find your *Microwave Magic* set an invaluable source of information and ideas that will enable you to get the most out of your microwave oven.

Power Levels

All the recipes in this series have been tested in a 700 watt oven. As there are many microwave ovens on the market with different power levels, and as the names of these levels vary from one manufacturer to another, we have decided to give power levels as a percentage. To adapt the power levels given here, consult the chart opposite and the instruction manual for your oven.

Generally speaking, if you have a 500 watt or 600 watt oven you should increase cooking times by about 30% over those given, depending on the actual length of time required. The shorter the original cooking time, the greater the percentage by which it must be lengthened. The 30% figure is only an average. Consult the chart for detailed information on this topic.

Power Levels

HIGH: 100% - 90%	Vegetables (except boiled potatoes and carrots) Soup Sauce Fruits Browning ground beef Browning dish Popcorn
MEDIUM HIGH: 80% - 70%	Rapid defrosting of precooked dishes Muffins Some cakes Hot dogs
MEDIUM: 60% - 50%	Cooking tender meat Cakes Fish Seafood Eggs Reheating Boiled potatoes and carrots
MEDIUM LOW: 40%	Cooking less tender meat Simmering Melting chocolate
DEFROST: 30% **LOW: 30% - 20%**	Defrosting Simmering Cooking less tender meat
WARM: 10%	Keeping food warm Allowing yeast dough to rise

Cooking Time Conversion Chart

700 watts	600 watts*
5 s	11 s
15 s	20 s
30 s	40 s
45 s	1 min
1 min	1 min 20 s
2 min	2 min 40 s
3 min	4 min
4 min	5 min 20 s
5 min	6 min 40 s
6 min	8 min
7 min	9 min 20 s
8 min	10 min 40 s
9 min	12 min
10 min	13 min 30 s
20 min	26 min 40 s
30 min	40 min
40 min	53 min 40 s
50 min	66 min 40 s
1 h	1 h 20 min

* There is very little difference in cooking times between 500 watt ovens and 600 watt ovens.

Special Characteristics of the Microwave Oven

The microwave oven is not as recent an invention as is generally supposed. In fact, American research into radar in the late 1940s resulted in the development and trial of the first microwave oven prototypes. The first such domestic appliances appeared on the market around 1955 and microwave ovens gradually gained a reputation for the speed with which they cooked food. Their growing popularity raised many questions, both about their functional value and about the effect of their specific type of energy on human health—questions that led to extensive research. Experts have since established that normal use of the microwave oven does not pose any risk. On the contrary, this type of quick cooking is more effective in maintaining the nutritional value in food than is conventional cooking. In light of these encouraging results, public mistrust has dissipated and the microwave has gained well-deserved popularity.

But what exactly are these microwaves? They are short waves, similar to the ordinary radio waves that surround us daily, but with a much more limited range. Like radio waves, microwaves pass through certain materials without affecting them; they penetrate porcelain, glass, certain plastics, paper and cardboard without increasing the temperature of these materials.

However, microwaves very quickly agitate the water, fat and sugar molecules which are present in almost all foods. Microwaves exert an electromagnetic force which ranges from positive to negative along a 2.45 megahertz cycle and which causes these molecules to spin at a rate of almost 2-1/2 million times per second. The high speed of agitation and the resulting friction from the molecules rubbing against each other produces sufficient heat to cook almost any food rapidly. This heat production is similar to the friction that results from rubbing one hand against the other but is much more intense. In other words, the foods themselves produce the heat required for their own cooking.

Microwaves may be compared to radio waves but they are quite distinct from other types of waves, such as X-rays and ultraviolet rays, which do entail certain risks for humans. These latter waves have an ionizing effect that produces irreversible chemical changes in living cells without perceptibly altering their temperature. Their effect on living cells is also cumulative. Microwaves, on the other hand, cannot be stored and are clearly perceived by our bodies as an intense heat. So, we can be sure that we are never eating microwaves by consuming foods prepared in this way, even though we commonly, but incorrectly, say that foods *absorb* microwaves.

Microwaves spread within the oven in a specific way; they first heat the food on the periphery of the dish and then gradually spread toward the food in the center. The microwaves very quickly heat the molecules in the bones and juices of meat, poultry, etc. Unlike the traditional oven, the microwave oven heats only the food. The oven walls, the rack (several models of ovens are equipped with a plastic rack) and even the dishes in which the foods cook are not directly affected by the microwaves. Of course, a dish may be hot when taken out of the oven, but the reason for this lies in the fact that the food's internal heat has been slowly transmitted to the dish.

The heat produced by a heating element is beneficial for roasting and for cooking certain recipes, such as puff pastry. For this reason, there are many ovens on the market that combine microwave and convection features. These appliances are equipped with a magnetron to generate microwaves and a heating element that emits forced heat from a ventilator. Alternating these two methods of cooking is a perfect way of quickly preparing certain types of food.

Microwave Cooking Accessories

The Microwave Rack
Some models of microwave ovens are equipped with an adjustable rack. This accessory has two main functions. First, it promotes a more rapid and even cooking of certain foods by allowing the microwaves to reach the food from below. The microwave rack is made of plastic which allows for the penetration of the microwaves; they can thus pass through the food in all directions for maximum effectiveness. Second, it increases the oven's capacity by allowing for the placement of more dishes in the oven. So, to cook or reheat more than one dish at a time, place the fastest cooking dishes on the bottom of the oven and the slower cooking ones on the rack. Of course, the greater the quantity of food, the longer the cooking of reheating time.

The Thermometer
We all know how useful it is to have a thermometer when cooking candy, milk-based recipes, large roasts or poultry. But few people know that the thermometer can also be used to monitor the temperature of soup or a hot beverage. There are two types of thermometers: those with no metal parts which can be used during microwave cooking and those which have metal parts and are used in conventional cooking. The latter should

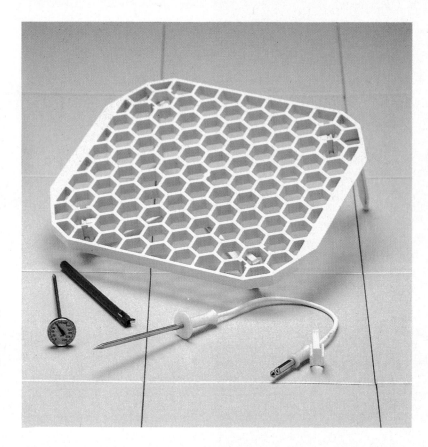

The microwave rack is made of plastic. The thermometer monitors the degree of doneness of several types of food. The temperature probe interrupts the cooking process when the food's internal temperature is sufficiently high.

never be left in a working microwave oven since there is a risk of it reflecting the microwaves toward the magnetron and causing damage to the oven. Of course, there is no risk in using this type of thermometer to check the internal temperature of food once it is outside the oven.

The Temperature Probe
Several models of microwave ovens are equipped with a temperature probe, or tuning fork. This device is similar to a thermometer in that it measures the internal temperature of the food but it also transmits this information through a wire

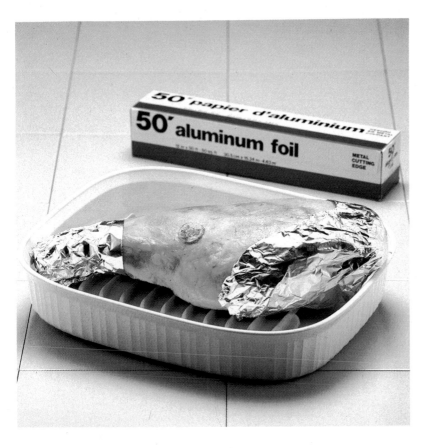

Aluminum foil protects food from overcooking and reduces heat loss during standing time outside the oven. Plastic wrap and waxed paper retain moisture and thus accelerate cooking and reheating.

reflective properties protect those parts that may be overexposed to the microwaves during defrosting, cooking or reheating as well as reduce heat loss during the required standing time.

Aluminum foil is used as a screen to decelerate the effect of the microwaves on the more vulnerable parts of certain foods. We know that the microwaves defrost and cook the bony parts of poultry and meat more quickly than the fleshy parts. The breastbone and the ends of the drumsticks of poultry and the bony parts of chops, steaks and ham tend to defrost and cook more quickly than other parts. To ensure that defrosting and cooking are uniform, cover these parts with aluminum foil before putting the meat or poultry into the oven. In the same way, thinner and irregular pieces of meat should be covered, as should the heads and tails of whole fish, to prevent them from drying out during defrosting or cooking.

The ends of roasts should also be covered with aluminum foil during cooking, as should the ends of dishes containing meat loaf and the corners of square molds when cooking certain foods, such as cakes. The reason for this precaution is that the corners

to the oven's control panel. Thus, when the center of the food reaches the pre-selected temperature the oven automatically shuts off. This accessory is very useful, not only for cooking roasts and poultry but also for perfect monitoring during the reheating process, for cooking small pieces of meat

and for heating liquids as well. For best results, the probe must be placed at the center of the food.

Aluminum Foil

Aluminum foil, a convenient accessory for microwave cooking, is the only metallic substance that can be used with microwaves. Its

of dishes are doubly exposed to the microwaves and are therefore particularly vulnerable to drying out.

It should be noted, however, that some caution is required in the use of aluminum foil. Do not use more than necessary so as not to hamper the circulation of the microwaves. And never let the aluminum foil touch the sides of the oven.

As previously mentioned, aluminum foil is also used as an insulator during the standing time, which is the last stage of microwave cooking. It can be used to cover roasts, dishes with sauces or to completely cover certain foods, such as baked potatoes. In this way, the food's internal heat continues to increase without the surface cooling off.

To ensure uniform cooking and to prevent overcooking the less fleshy parts of poultry, cover the wings, the tips of the drumsticks and the backbone with aluminum foil.

Use aluminum foil to cover the corners of square molds when cooking cakes.

Aluminum foil can also be used as an insulator during the standing time, which is the last stage of the microwave cooking process.

Plastic Wrap, Waxed Paper and Paper Towel

Plastic wrap is mainly used to cover food being cooked in containers that do not have lids, such as platters, loaf dishes and baking dishes. Place the plastic wrap carefully around the edges of the dish, leaving a gap for excess steam to escape. Since part of the steam is captured, cooking is more rapid and there is less danger of the food drying out.

Waxed paper is also used to prevent dehydration, mainly during reheating, although it is less effective than plastic wrap. It can also be used to protect the inside of the oven against spattering.

The absorbent qualities of paper towel make it an ideal screen to protect against spattering. It can be used to cover certain greasy foods, such as bacon and sausages, during cooking.

Plastic wrap is used to cover food cooked in dishes without lids, such as platters, loaf dishes and baking dishes.

Waxed paper is used to prevent dehydration, especially during reheating.

The absorbent qualities of paper towel make it an ideal screen against spattering.

The Timer

Even though the microwave oven is equipped with a very precise timer, an independent timer is a useful reminder for cooks who prepare several recipes at once—reminding them when various steps in the recipe should be carried out, keeping track of the standing times for different dishes and so on.

Oven Mitts and Pot Holders

It is well known that microwaves directly heat only the food and not its container. However, when food becomes hot, the heat is transmitted to the dish in which it is cooked. This is especially true when the food cooks for a long time in the oven or for foods with sauces that fill more than two thirds of the dish. It is therefore always prudent to use oven mitts or pot holders.

Utensils for Measurement and Preparation

Measuring Cups and Spoons

To measure liquids, granular substances or powders, use measuring cups and a set of measuring spoons. The best measuring cups are transparent, oven safe and equipped with a lip and spout. Using a transparent cup makes it easy to check the exact level of the product by setting the cup at eye level on a flat surface. The lip and spout prevent liquids from spilling when adding them to other ingredients in a given recipe. Furthermore, since the cup is marked with both metric and imperial measures, you can make any recipe without having to convert the ingredient quantities.

To precisely measure small quantities of liquids, grains or powders, two sets of measuring spoons, one metric and one imperial, are indispensable. Never substitute ordinary cutlery or dishes (teaspoons, tablespoons, cups, etc.) when measuring because their volume varies greatly from one manufacturer to another.

The Kitchen Scale

Many cook books, particularly European ones, specify ingredients such as flour, sugar, butter and so on, by weight and not by volume. Such ingredients as meat, fish and poultry are also almost always measured by weight. You will then find that a kitchen scale, sensitive enough to measure very small quantities and marked with both metric and imperial measurements, will be very useful.

Culinary art is closely linked to food chemistry. For this reason appropriate utensils

for measurement and preparation are essential for successful recipes. Ingredient volumes are measured with measuring cups or a set of measuring spoons, depending on the quantity. A kitchen scale is useful when the amount of a required

ingredient is indicated in weight.

Other principal utensils with which a kitchen should be equipped include: an assortment of good quality knives and a chopping board, a vegetable brush and a mushroom brush, a vegetable peeler, a grater with various sizes of holes, a grinder, a set of mixing bowls, wooden spoons and a whisk. Other useful utensils include a plastic colander, a metal colander, a sieve, a mortar and pestle, a potato masher and an electric mixer.

During everyday cooking we sometimes tend to neglect some procedures that seem overly simple. However, it is often these procedures that make or break a recipe. Accurate measurement is the most important of these simple but sometimes neglected procedures. Frequently satisfied with approximate guesses, we do not realize the effect that these small variations in quantity may have on the taste, texture or appearance of the final product, particularly with delicate recipes, such as some desserts. Using the right measuring utensils and measuring carefully are essential steps.

Knives and Chopping Boards

How often have you searched through your kitchen drawers, desperately looking for a knife that will cut properly? It is extremely important to be equipped with a good quality set of knives and a good steel to maintain them. Knives are truly indispensable kitchen utensils.

Even the simplest culinary operations are difficult to execute with one single knife. You cannot peel vegetables with a knife used to slice roasts or slice bread with a knife meant for filleting fish.

Furthermore, all these operations can be carried out safely, for both yourself and your counters, if the food to be sliced or chopped is carefully placed on a good chopping board.

Vegetable Brushes and Mushroom Brushes

Most fruits and vegetables taste better and maintain more of their nutritional value if they are served with their skin. To thoroughly clean the surface of fresh fruits and vegetables, removing all traces of earth, sand, dust and insecticide, the best and perhaps the oldest method is to scrub the fruit or vegetable with a vegetable brush under running water. To clean those vegetables and fruits having a more fragile skin, such as zucchini or pears, it is best to use a mushroom brush. This brush is more supple than a vegetable brush and won't scratch the skin.

Remember that mushrooms should never be washed. Their skin is very porous and absorbent and even a simple rinsing will reduce their flavor; therefore, brush the mushrooms with a proper mushroom brush.

Remember too that it is always best to wash fruits and vegetables just before using them. By not washing them ahead of time, they maintain their freshness and flavor longer.

The Peeler, Grater and Grinder

It is quite difficult to peel some vegetables with a paring knife. For example, peeling an uneven carrot or a large rutabaga is awkward without a vegetable peeler. This utensil removes an even layer of skin all over and reduces the risk of cuts.

A well-equipped kitchen should also have different sizes of graters with different sizes of holes. A grater with large holes can be used to shred cabbage, for example. Graters with medium-sized and small holes are appropriate for grating certain vegetables or cheeses and a small grater with tiny holes is used to grate tough food products, such as nutmeg.

A grinder is not essential if you have only a small quantity of food to grind. However, it will save you a great deal of time if you frequently grind large quantities of food.

Mixing Bowls, Wooden Spoons and Whisks

Preparing a mixture without spilling is easy if you use a bowl that is much larger than the quantity of its contents. If you have an entire set of mixing bowls, you will always be sure to have the size you need. Extra large measuring cups can also be used as mixing bowls.

Wooden spoons, of different lengths for different quantities to be mixed, are used to gently stir ingredients without scratching the bowls.

A whisk is essential to beat mixtures that require the addition of a great deal of air—egg whites, for example. If the quantity is very large, use an electric hand mixer instead. The whisk is also an extremely useful utensil to avoid lumping when mixing flour-based sauces or gravies.

Colanders and Sieves

The colander is used to wash and drain foods as well as to filter certain liquids, such as stocks. Depending on the intended use, choose a plastic colander or one made of metal. The plastic colander is best for rinsing acidic fruits, their taste being easily altered by metal. It can also be used as a cooking utensil in the microwave oven; ground meat cooked in a plastic colander placed on a dish will be almost fat free. Metal colanders are stronger and are therefore best for filtering liquids and sauces; the mixture being filtered can be easily pressed through the holes with a pestle or the back of a spoon.

Finally, the sieve is meant to sift and evenly combine such dry ingredients as flour, baking soda, sugar, salt, pepper and so on. It is also used to strain sauces and other liquids to eliminate any curdled or inedible substances.

The Mortar and Pestle

These two utensils are inseparable and, in fact, are often considered as one. They are indispensable for grinding and mixing several ingredients or for crushing a single ingredient into powder (dried herbs, spices, nuts, cooked vegetables, fruits, cooked meat and poultry, seafood, etc.). The mortar and pestle have many more uses than is generally supposed.

Utensils for Cooking and Reheating

Serving Forks and Tongs

Serving forks and tongs are invaluable for rearranging pieces of food or turning them over during cooking. The serving fork is mainly used to manipulate large cuts of meat like roasts or ham and to hold them firmly while carving. It can also be helpful in checking the doneness of meat.

Tongs facilitate the handling of foods such as bacon, sausages and cutlets. Since these utensils are made of metal, it is obvious that they should never be left in the microwave oven.

Spatulas

Spatulas are used to manipulate most types of flat foods and to keep them from sticking. With a thin, stiff spatula it is easy to move or turn steaks, meat patties and eggs over without breaking them. To prevent scratching the bottom of pyrex or porcelain dishes, use a plastic spatula rather than a metal one. A pointed spatula is ideal for serving slices of pie, tart or pâté.

Spoons and Ladles

Spoons used to mix or stir foods are very different from the spoons in your everyday cutlery. The former are usually narrow, shallow and made of wood or plastic so as not to scratch cooking dishes. The latter are often more elegant and much deeper. The ladle is the best utensil to use when serving soup.

Baster

The baster is a simple but ingenious utensil, well known by cooks who often prepare roasts or poultry. It consists of a large dropper with a suction cup at the top and is used to draw the cooking juices from the bottom of the dish and then to squeeze them over the cut of meat. This utensil is more than just a gadget when you consider the inconvenience of using a ladle or a small spoon, not to mention the risk of burns.

Dishes for Cooking and Reheating

Cooking dishes can be rectangular, square, round or oval. They are mainly made of pyrex or porcelain and some have low sides. Dishes without lids can be covered, if needed, with plastic wrap but be sure to leave one corner open so that excess steam can escape. Except for large platters, most microwave dishes are equipped with two handles.

Square Dishes

Square dishes are mainly used to cook such solid foods as steaks, meat patties, cutlets or roasts. They are less suitable for cooking foods with sauces because the microwaves tend to overcook the food in the corners. This problem can be avoided, however, by covering each corner with a piece of aluminum foil.

Round and Oval Dishes

Round and oval dishes are the most appropriate dishes for the microwave. They can be used for all types of foods, both solid and liquid. Because their shape corresponds to the distribution of microwaves in the oven, they are best for ensuring even cooking.

The Casserole Dish

The casserole is a deep dish with a cover and is ideal for braising. It allows excess steam to escape while retaining most of the food's moisture. It is used to cook foods that dry out easily to prepare those that require slow cooking.

The Browning Dish

The main purpose of the browning dish is to sear food in butter or oil before cooking but it is frequently used for roasting as well.

This square dish is equipped with sides and handles and is the only dish that becomes heated when in contact with the microwaves. The bottom of the browning dish is coated with a special substance, usually ferrite, which does absorb microwaves and becomes very hot. After heating the browning dish for a few minutes in the oven it is capable of searing food outside the oven. Never put the browning dish on a plastic rack in the oven, as the rack would melt.

Roasting Bags

The roasting bag, like the casserole, can be used to braise food and shares many of the advantages of the casserole. Be sure to leave an opening in the bag to allow excess steam to escape, otherwise the bag will explode. And never use a metal tie to close the bag.

The Ring Dish (or Tube Pan)

Its round shape and center tube make this dish ideal for fast and uniform cooking. As well, the defrosting of food, such as ground meat, which has been frozen in the ring dish is simplified because there is no food in the center, where defrosting takes longer.

The Bacon Rack

Because microwaves rapidly heat liquids and cooking juices that escape from food, it is important that the food does not come into contact with its liquid during defrosting or cooking, or neither process would be uniform. The bacon rack, with its grooved surface, is therefore ideal for defrosting or cooking bacon, ground beef patties, cutlets, steaks, pieces of fish and many other foods that release juices when heated.

The Rack

This rectangular rack serves much the same purpose as the bacon rack. It is used to defrost large pieces of meat and it is usually placed in the bottom of a large dish to collect the juices released from large cuts of meat during roasting.

Glass Cake Molds

Round cake molds give the best results in the microwave oven. The cake batter cooks more evenly and, if the dish is transparent, you can check for doneness simply by looking through the bottom. When using square molds, cover the corners with aluminum foil to prevent overcooking the batter which, at the corners, is doubly exposed to the microwaves.

Muffin Pans

Muffin pans designed for use in the microwave oven are usually made of plastic and contain six cups arranged in a circle. They do not have one in the center since, there, the batter would cook more slowly than that around the periphery of the pan.

Plastic Containers

Plastic containers that are microwave safe and that can be hermetically sealed are available in all shapes and sizes. These containers are ideal for storing and defrosting food because they can be taken from the freezer and put directly into the microwave oven for defrosting. Be sure, however, to open the lid to prevent the pressure of the steam from causing the container to explode. It should also be noted that plastic containers are quickly heated by the food they contain and are therefore not suitable for cooking.

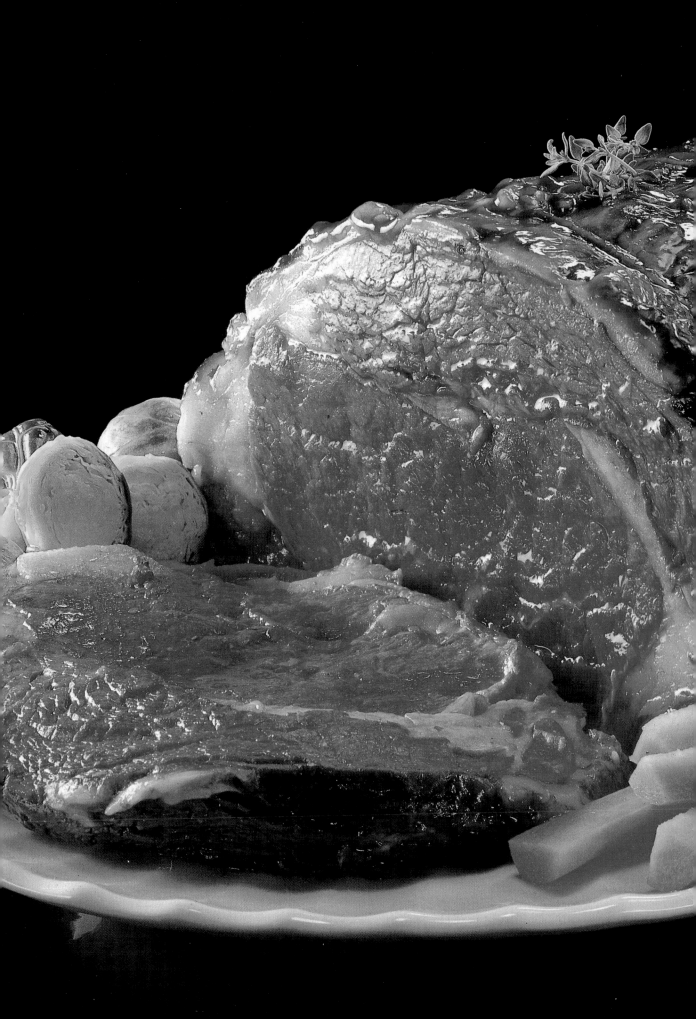

Alphabetical Index

All-purpose ground beef base	Vol. 14 p.	24
All-purpose pork base	Vol. 4 p.	92
All-purpose turkey base	Vol. 14 p.	28
Almond (Chantilly—cream)	Vol. 22 p.	96
Almond cookies	Vol. 18 p.	88
Almond cream	Vol. 3 p.	102
Almonds (Asparagus with)	Vol. 13 p.	90
Almonds (Beef tongue with)	Vol. 8 p.	76
Almonds (Broccoli with)	Vol. 13 p.	58
Almonds (Peaches stuffed with— and raisins)	Vol. 19 p.	92
Almonds (Pickerel stuffed with green grapes and)	Vol. 5 p.	50
Almonds (Rice with)	Vol. 12 p.	83
Almonds (Scallops with)	Vol. 14 p.	92
Almonds (Trout with)	Vol. 24 p.	22
Anchovy sauce	Vol. 11 p.	42
Antilles eggs	Vol. 25 p.	54
Appetizers (Cold sauces for cold)	Vol. 15 p.	14
Appetizers (Preparing hot)	Vol. 15 p.	12
Apple and coconut Brown Betty	Vol. 9 p.	50
Apple and raisin cake	Vol. 19 p.	90
Apple (Baked)	Vol. 20 p.	98
Apple compote	Vol. 9 p.	88
Apple crepes	Vol. 9 p.	99
Apple crisp	Vol. 3 p.	103
Apple crumble	Vol. 9 p.	72
Apple (Curried—soup)	Vol. 25 p.	32
Apple omelette	Vol. 20 p.	78
Apple omelette flambé	Vol. 16 p.	38
Apple pie	Vol. 3 p.	86
Apple quick bread	Vol. 9 p.	25
Apple (Sausages with—slices)	Vol. 4 p.	88
Apple spice bread	Vol. 3 p.	36
Apples (Caramel)	Vol. 9 p.	48
Apples (Duck with)	Vol. 17 p.	48
Apples (Goose with)	Vol. 17 p.	60
Apples (Lamb chops with)	Vol. 10 p.	78
Apples (Veal rump roast with)	Vol. 10 p.	30
Apples with Gruyère cheese	Vol. 23 p.	27
Applesauce	Vol. 11 p.	54
Applesauce cookies	Vol. 9 p.	49
Apricot cookies	Vol. 21 p.	98
Apricot flan	Vol. 10 p.	105
Apricots (Chicken with)	Vol. 19 p.	58
Apricots (Crown roast of lamb with)	Vol. 10 p.	72
Artichoke and mushroom salad	Vol. 13 p.	86
Artichoke bottoms with two stuffings	Vol. 15 p.	50
Artichoke (Cream of cucumber and—soup)	Vol. 11 p.	72
Artichokes (Casserole of—and peas)	Vol. 13 p.	83
Artichokes (Stuffed)	Vol. 13 p.	84
Asparagus (Cream of—soup)	Vol. 5 p.	100
Asparagus on toast	Vol. 23 p.	30
Asparagus (Poached eggs on—mousse)	Vol. 23 p.	40
Asparagus with almonds	Vol. 13 p.	90
Asparagus with Mornay or Béarnaise sauce	Vol. 15 p.	54
Asparagus with mustard sauce	Vol. 4 p.	101
Aspic (Delicious)	Vol. 25 p.	22
Aspic (Duck in)	Vol. 18 p.	34
Avocado (Turkey-stuffed)	Vol. 14 p.	50
Avocado with cream cheese and nuts	Vol. 15 p.	78
Avocados with seafood	Vol. 15 p.	98

B

Bacon (Beef with celery and)	Vol. 1 p.	**54**
Bacon (Sausages and)	Vol. 23 p.	**80**
Bacon (Turkey and—croquettes)	Vol. 2 p.	**36**
Baked apple	Vol. 20 p.	**98**
Baked beans with partridge	Vol. 17 p.	**36**
Baked potatoes	Vol. 13 p.	**32**
Baked potatoes in their jackets	Vol. 20 p.	**98**
Banana cake	Vol. 3 p.	**54**
Banana crepes	Vol. 9 p.	**98**
Banana (Whole wheat—bread)	Vol. 3 p.	**34**
Barbecue sauce	Vol. 11 p.	**48**
Barley and vegetable soup	Vol. 11 p.	**86**
Bass (Steamed—with black beans)	Vol. 18 p.	**56**
Bean (Broad—soup)	Vol. 19 p.	**24**
Beans (Baked—with partridge)	Vol. 17 p.	**36**
Beans (Boston baked)	Vol. 24 p.	**96**
Beans (Frankfurters and)	Vol. 8 p.	**96**
Beans (Lamb chops with)	Vol. 19 p.	**70**
Beans (Meatballs with baked)	Vol. 8 p.	**61**
Beans (Navy—with pineapple)	Vol. 21 p.	**46**
Beans (Yellow—Creole style)	Vol. 13 p.	**61**
Bear (Roast)	Vol. 17 p.	**92**
Bear stew	Vol. 17 p.	**94**
Béarnaise sauce	Vol. 1 p.	**35**
Béchamel sauce	Vol. 11 p.	**13**
Béchamel sauce with peppers	Vol. 11 p.	**28**
Beef à la mode	Vol. 8 p.	**30**
Beef (All-purpose ground—base)	Vol. 14 p.	**24**
Beef and macaroni casserole with corn	Vol. 14 p.	**32**
Beef and peppers	Vol. 18 p.	**100**
Beef (Bologna and—rolls)	Vol. 22 p.	**26**
Beef Bourguignon (Double recipe)	Vol. 1 p.	**56**
Beef Bourguignon (Single recipe)	Vol. 22 p.	**38**
Beef (Braised)	Vol. 1 p.	**66**
Beef (Cheesy—pie)	Vol. 8 p.	**64**
Beef (Chinese—casserole)	Vol. 14 p.	**34**
Beef (Chinese) *with sake*	Vol. 1 p.	**52**
Beef (Chinese) *with soy sauce*	Vol. 21 p.	**62**
Beef (Curried)	Vol. 14 p.	**30**
Beef flank	Vol. 8 p.	**42**
Beef goulash	Vol. 8 p.	**83**
Beef (Ground—base)	Vol. 1 p.	**90**
Beef (Ground—casserole) *with green beans*	Vol. 1 p.	**72**
Beef (Ground—casserole) *with potatoes and carrots*	Vol. 22 p.	**40**
Beef (Ground—stew)	Vol. 8 p.	**56**
Beef heart (Stuffed)	Vol. 8 p.	**105**
Beef in beer	Vol. 1 p.	**58**
Beef in patty shells	Vol. 8 p.	**92**
Beef kebabs	Vol. 1 p.	**60**
Beef kidneys	Vol. 8 p.	**80**
Beef (Lentil and ground—casserole)	Vol. 21 p.	**64**
Beef liver in brown gravy	Vol. 1 p.	**96**
Beef (Macédoine of)	Vol. 1 p.	**45**
Beef (Mexican)	Vol. 8 p.	**84**
Beef (Mexican—stew)	Vol. 19 p.	**66**
Beef (New England braised)	Vol. 8 p.	**28**
Beef Niçoise	Vol. 8 p.	**94**
Beef (Oriental—with mandarins)	Vol. 8 p.	**50**
Beef ramekins	Vol. 1 p.	**76**
Beef (Roast)	Vol. 25 p.	**66**
Beef (Roast—with herbs)	Vol. 8 p.	**22**
Beef (Roast—with mustard sauce)	Vol. 23 p.	**72**

Beef roulades	Vol. 24 p. **40**
Beef roulades with mustard	Vol. 1 p. **48**
Beef salad	Vol. 14 p. **76**
Beef sausages	Vol. 8 p. **74**
Beef sauté with orange segments	Vol. 19 p. **68**
Beef soup	Vol. 21 p. **26**
Beef (Spicy—soup)	Vol. 24 p. **72**
Beef Stroganoff	Vol. 1 p. **40**
Beef surprise with yoghurt	Vol. 8 p. **53**
Beef tenderloin marinated in soy sauce	Vol. 1 p. **102**
Beef tongue with almonds	Vol. 8 p. **76**
Beef Wellington	Vol. 8 p. **46**
Beef with celery and bacon	Vol. 1 p. **54**
Beef with olives	Vol. 1 p. **68**
Beef with orange	Vol. 22 p. **34**
Beef with red peppers	Vol. 8 p. **48**
Beef with sliced peppers	Vol. 8 p. **78**
Beer (Beef in)	Vol. 1 p. **58**
Beer (Ham in)	Vol. 23 p. **22**
Beer (Hare with)	Vol. 17 p. **100**
Beet ketchup	Vol. 13 p. **49**
Beets (Harvard)	Vol. 19 p. **48**
Beets julienne	Vol. 23 p. **50**
Beets with vinegar	Vol. 13 p. **48**
Black beans (Steamed bass with)	Vol. 18 p. **56**
Black cherries (Cornish game hens with)	Vol. 7 p. **62**
Black forest cake	Vol. 25 p. **28**
Black magic pudding	Vol. 9 p. **69**
Blade roast	Vol. 8 p. **40**
Blanquette of veal	Vol. 10 p. **52**
Blueberries with yoghurt and honey	Vol. 23 p. **37**
Blueberry jam	Vol. 9 p. **95**
Blueberry pie	Vol. 24 p. **105**
Bologna and beef rolls	Vol. 22 p. **26**
Boneless shoulder roast	Vol. 8 p. **24**
Bordelaise sauce	Vol. 1 p. **34**
Boston baked beans	Vol. 24 p. **96**
Boston cream cake	Vol. 9 p. **42**
Boston lettuce with tarragon vinegar	Vol. 23 p. **100**
Bouillabaise	Vol. 5 p. **54**
Bourbon mousse	Vol. 25 p. **70**

Braised beef	Vol. 1 **p.**	**66**
Braised lamb chops with vegetables	Vol. 10 **p.**	**82**
Braised lamb liver	Vol. 10 **p.**	**92**
Braised tuna	Vol. 24 **p.**	**84**
Braised turkey with vegetables	Vol. 2 **p.**	**26**
Braised veal shank	Vol. 10 **p.**	**36**
Braised vegetables	Vol. 19 **p.**	**40**
Bran (Date and—muffins)	Vol. 23 **p.**	**66**
Bran muffins with molasses	Vol. 23 **p.**	**76**
Brandy (Goose with pears in)	Vol. 7 **p.**	**34**
Bread (Cranberry)	Vol. 19 **p.**	**100**
Bread (Garlic)	Vol. 22 **p.**	**28**
Bread (Poppy seed)	Vol. 3 **p.**	**33**
Bread pudding	Vol. 9 **p.**	**70**
Bread sauce	Vol. 11 **p.**	**28**
Bread (Stuffed)	Vol. 25 **p.**	**20**
Bread (Whole wheat)	Vol. 3 **p.**	**32**
Bread (Whole wheat banana)	Vol. 3 **p.**	**34**
Breakfast buns	Vol. 9 **p.**	**26**
Broad bean soup	Vol. 19 **p.**	**24**
Broccoli and cheese casserole	Vol. 23 **p.**	**50**
Broccoli and cheese quiche	Vol. 16 **p.**	**86**
Broccoli and ham casserole	Vol. 13 **p.**	**56**
Broccoli and ham rolls	Vol. 25 **p.**	**44**
Broccoli and onion soup	Vol. 19 **p.**	**30**
Broccoli (Chicken and—quiche)	Vol. 2 **p.**	**86**
Broccoli (Chicken with)	Vol. 18 **p.**	**30**
Broccoli (Cream of leek and—soup)	Vol. 21 **p.**	**36**
Broccoli (Ground pork with)	Vol. 18 **p.**	**48**
Broccoli (Halibut fillets with)	Vol. 5 **p.**	**86**
Broccoli terrine	Vol. 21 **p.**	**42**
Broccoli with almonds	Vol. 13 **p.**	**58**
Broccoli with white wine	Vol. 21 **p.**	**48**
Broths (Compound)	Vol. 11 **p.**	**82**
Brown rice and mushroom salad	Vol. 12 **p.**	**101**
Brown sauce	Vol. 11 **p.**	**48**
Brussels sprouts with mushrooms	Vol. 13 **p.**	**59**
Brussels sprouts with sour cream	Vol. 13 **p.**	**60**
Buns (Hot cross)	Vol. 9 **p.**	**30**
Burbot with lemon butter	Vol. 5 **p.**	**83**
Burgundy Pheasant	Vol. 17 **p.**	**38**
Butter and dill sauce	Vol. 11 **p.**	**18**

C

Cabbage au gratin	Vol. 15 p. 70
Cabbage leaves stuffed with chicken	Vol. 2 p. 90
Cabbage (Partridge with)	Vol. 17 p. 34
Cabbage quiche	Vol. 13 p. 54
Cabbage (Roast veal shoulder with)	Vol. 10 p. 24
Cabbage rolls	Vol. 24 p. 48
Cabbage soup	Vol. 11 p. 93
Cabbage (Stuffed—rolls)	Vol. 1 p. 70
Cake (Apple and raisin)	Vol. 19 p. 90
Cake (Banana)	Vol. 3 p. 54
Cake (Black forest)	Vol. 25 p. 28
Cake (Boston cream)	Vol. 9 p. 42
Cake (Carrot)	Vol. 1 p. 105
Cake (Chocolate chip)	Vol. 23 p. 86
Cake (Chocolate fudge)	Vol. 3 p. 64
Cake (Fruit)	Vol. 3 p. 56
Cake (Jujube)	Vol. 25 p. 78
Cake (Mocha)	Vol. 25 p. 105
Cake (Orange crown)	Vol. 25 p. 60
Cake (Peanut butter)	Vol. 9 p. 38
Cake (Pineapple)	Vol. 3 p. 52
Cake (Queen Elizabeth)	Vol. 3 p. 62
Cake (Strawberry-lime chiffon)	Vol. 23 p. 36
Cake (Strawberry short—)	Vol. 22 p. 92
Cake (Tomato)	Vol. 9 p. 44
Cake (White)	Vol. 3 p. 55
Calf's brains	Vol. 10 p. 58
Calf's liver	Vol. 10 p. 34
Camembert fritters	Vol. 16 p. 70
Canadian ham	Vol. 4 p. 40
Cannelloni with veal and spinach	Vol. 12 p. 50
Caper sauce	Vol. 11 p. 25
Capers (Trout with)	Vol. 22 p. 104
Captain's plate	Vol. 6 p. 104
Caramel and cherry ring	Vol. 9 p. 32
Caramel apples	Vol. 9 p. 48
Caramel cream	Vol. 3 p. 82
Caribou meat loaf	Vol. 17 p. 90
Caribou (Roast)	Vol. 17 p. 88
Carrot cake	Vol. 1 p. 105
Carrot (Cream of—soup) *beef stock*	Vol. 25 p. 74
Carrot (Cream of—soup) *chicken stock*	Vol. 12 p. 100

Carrot soup	Vol. 21 p. 32
Carrots Basque	Vol. 15 p. 56
Carrots (Chicken with—in sesame sauce)	Vol. 24 p. 70
Carrots (Glazed)	Vol. 13 p. 45
Carrots (Glazed) *with honey and ginger*	Vol. 20 p. 32
Carrots (Vichy)	Vol. 25 p. 27
Carrots with cream	Vol. 13 p. 46
Casserole (Beef and macaroni—with corn)	Vol. 14 p. 32
Casserole (Broccoli and ham)	Vol. 13 p. 56
Casserole (Chicken) *whole chicken*	Vol. 14 p. 84
Casserole (Chicken) *chicken pieces*	Vol. 7 p. 94
Casserole (Chicken and rice)	Vol. 18 p. 80
Casserole (Chinese beef)	Vol. 14 p. 34
Casserole (Crabmeat)	Vol. 6 p. 61
Casserole (Ground beef)	Vol. 1 p. 72
Casserole (Ham and macaroni)	Vol. 14 p. 95
Casserole (Hare)	Vol. 17 p. 98
Casserole (Lentil and ground beef)	Vol. 21 p. 64
Casserole of artichokes and peas	Vol. 13 p. 83
Casserole (Onion and tomato)	Vol. 13 p. 78
Casserole (Quail—with peas)	Vol. 7 p. 61
Casserole (Rice and vegetable)	Vol. 12 p. 88
Casserole (Seafood)	Vol. 6 p. 88
Casserole (Turkey and cheese)	Vol. 14 p. 52
Casserole (Veal)	Vol. 10 p. 28
Cassoulet	Vol. 24 p. 18
Cauliflower à la Polonaise	Vol. 13 p. 60
Cauliflower au gratin	Vol. 1 p. 103
Cauliflower (Cream of—soup)	Vol. 11 p. 66
Cauliflower (Mushroom and—salad)	Vol. 22 p. 101
Cauliflower quiche	Vol. 15 p. 72
Celery (Beef with—and bacon)	Vol. 1 p. 54
Celery (Chicken stuffed with—and nuts)	Vol. 2 p. 50
Celery (Cream of—soup)	Vol. 6 p. 101
Celery soup	Vol. 19 p. 34
Champagne (Chicken in)	Vol. 7 p. 76
Champagne punch	Vol. 23 p. 104
Chantilly cream with almonds	Vol. 23 p. 105
Cheddar (Macaroni with—cheese)	Vol. 12 p. 61

Alphabetical Index

Cheese and rice loaf	Vol. 16 p.	96
Cheese and tomato flan	Vol. 16 p.	92
Cheese ball	Vol. 16 p.	68
Cheese (Broccoli and—casserole)	Vol. 23 p.	50
Cheese (Broccoli and—quiche)	Vol. 16 p.	86
Cheese (Chicken stuffed with)	Vol. 19 p.	56
Cheese (Gnocchi with—and tomato sauce)	Vol. 15 p.	84
Cheese (Macaroni and)	Vol. 16 p.	82
Cheese (Macédoine of vegetables with)	Vol. 16 p.	74
Cheese muffins	Vol. 19 p.	88
Cheese (Potatoes stuffed with sour cream and)	Vol. 15 p.	102
Cheese (Rutabaga and green pepper with)	Vol. 13 p.	53
Cheese (Salmon and—loaf)	Vol. 14 p.	88
Cheese soup	Vol. 16 p.	76
Cheese tray	Vol. 23 p.	41
Cheese (Turkey and—casserole)	Vol. 14 p.	52
Cheesecake	Vol. 3 p.	58
Cheesecake (Mandarin)	Vol. 9 p.	40
Cheesecake (Tofu)	Vol. 21 p.	100
Cheesecakes (Individual)	Vol. 22 p.	94
Cheeses (Lasagna with four)	Vol. 12 p.	38
Cheesy beef pie	Vol. 8 p.	64
Cheesy pudding	Vol. 20 p.	52
Chef's salad	Vol. 4 p.	100
Cherry (Caramel and—ring)	Vol. 9 p.	32
Cherry jam	Vol. 9 p.	97
Cherry mousse	Vol. 9 p.	80
Chestnut mousse	Vol. 12 p.	105
Chick peas (Ratatouille with)	Vol. 19 p.	42
Chicken à la king	Vol. 2 p.	84
Chicken and broccoli quiche	Vol. 2 p.	86
Chicken and ham soup	Vol. 11 p.	84
Chicken and leek pie	Vol. 23 p.	54
Chicken and rice casserole	Vol. 18 p.	80
Chicken and rice soup	Vol. 11 p.	91
Chicken and rice vol-au-vents	Vol. 12 p.	96
Chicken breasts divan	Vol. 7 p.	80
Chicken breasts supreme *4 servings*	Vol. 2 p.	74
Chicken breasts supreme *10 servings*	Vol. 23 p.	32
Chicken breasts with peaches	Vol. 7 p.	82
Chicken breasts with pistachios	Vol. 7 p.	68
Chicken (Cabbage leaves stuffed with)	Vol. 2 p.	90
Chicken Cacciatore	Vol. 2 p.	94
Chicken casserole *chicken pieces*	Vol. 7 p.	94
Chicken casserole *whole chicken*	Vol. 14 p.	84
Chicken chasseur	Vol. 7 p.	92
Chicken (Couscous with—and shrimp)	Vol. 2 p.	96
Chicken croissant	Vol. 7 p.	84
Chicken divan	Vol. 20 p.	60
Chicken fricassee	Vol. 7 p.	90
Chicken (Garlic)	Vol. 23 p.	64
Chicken, ham and rice soup	Vol. 24 p.	83
Chicken (Honey-glazed)	Vol. 18 p.	24
Chicken (Hot—sandwich)	Vol. 7 p.	86
Chicken hotpot	Vol. 2 p.	82
Chicken in champagne	Vol. 7 p.	76
Chicken Italian style	Vol. 7 p.	72
Chicken kebabs	Vol. 23 p.	84
Chicken Kiev	Vol. 2 p.	48
Chicken (Lemon)	Vol. 2 p.	64

Alphabetical Index

Chicken (Lemon—with parsley)	Vol.	2 p.	78
Chicken liver and pork pâté	Vol.	15 p.	94
Chicken liver and rice soup	Vol.	11 p.	86
Chicken livers with noodles	Vol.	2 p.	68
Chicken Lo Chou	Vol.	18 p.	36
Chicken Madeira	Vol.	7 p.	78
Chicken (Marinated—kebabs)	Vol.	2 p.	70
Chicken (Mini—kebabs)	Vol.	15 p.	46
Chicken noodle soup	Vol.	11 p.	90
Chicken omelette	Vol.	2 p.	88
Chicken (Oriental)	Vol.	22 p.	46
Chicken Parmesan	Vol.	7 p.	70
Chicken paupiettes	Vol.	22 p.	48
Chicken pies	Vol.	7 p.	88
Chicken rice pilaf	Vol.	2 p.	59
Chicken (Rice with)	Vol.	12 p.	94
Chicken (Roast—with oregano)	Vol.	7 p.	74
Chicken rolls stuffed with crab	Vol.	22 p.	53
Chicken (Saffron)	Vol.	2 p.	52
Chicken salad	Vol.	2 p.	57
Chicken soup with snow peas	Vol.	18 p.	83
Chicken stock	Vol.	11 p.	58
Chicken (Stuffed roast)	Vol.	7 p.	45
Chicken stuffed with celery and nuts	Vol.	2 p.	50
Chicken stuffed with cheese	Vol.	19 p.	56
Chicken velouté sauce	Vol.	11 p.	28
Chicken wings with garlic	Vol.	2 p.	72
Chicken with apricots	Vol.	19 p.	58
Chicken with broccoli	Vol.	18 p.	30
Chicken with carrots in sesame sauce	Vol.	24 p.	70
Chicken with chili pepper and tomato sauce	Vol.	24 p.	76
Chicken with cumin	Vol.	22 p.	44
Chicken with dumplings	Vol.	2 p.	60
Chicken with garlic	Vol.	7 p.	66
Chicken with ginger	Vol.	2 p.	80
Chicken with orange	Vol.	2 p.	66
Chicken with peanuts	Vol.	18 p.	28
Chicken with pineapple	Vol.	18 p.	32
Chicken with sautéed vegetables	Vol.	7 p.	83
Chicken with sour cream	Vol.	7 p.	96
Chicken with white wine	Vol.	21 p.	56
Chicken with wine and herbs	Vol.	2 p.	62
Chicken with yoghurt	Vol.	21 p.	58
Chili	Vol.	1 p.	94
Chili pepper (Chicken with—and tomato sauce	Vol.	24 p.	76
Chinese beef *with soy sauce*	Vol.	21 p.	62
Chinese beef *with sake*	Vol.	1 p.	52
Chinese beef casserole	Vol.	14 p.	34
Chinese vegetables with oyster sauce	Vol.	18 p.	62
Chocolate chip cake	Vol.	23 p.	86
Chocolate chip cookies	Vol.	3 p.	24
Chocolate cream	Vol.	3 p.	82
Chocolate fondue	Vol.	3 p.	102
Chocolate frosting	Vol.	3 p.	69
Chocolate fudge	Vol.	20 p.	94
Chocolate fudge cake	Vol.	3 p.	64
Chocolate (Hot)	Vol.	23 p.	86
Chocolate Madrilène	Vol.	23 p.	66
Chocolate mint mousse	Vol.	9 p.	78
Chocolate mousse	Vol.	3 p.	101
Chocolate muffins	Vol.	3 p.	42

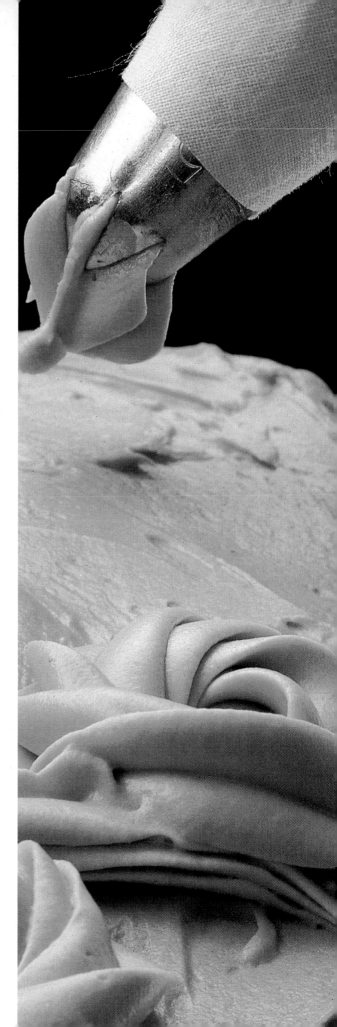

Chocolate topping	Vol. 3 p. 72	Crab (Chicken rolls stuffed with)	Vol. 22 p. 53
Chop suey with pork	Vol. 4 p. 96	Crab Florentine style	Vol. 6 p. 58
Chowder (Fish and zucchini)	Vol. 5 p. 56	Crab legs with lemon sauce	Vol. 6 p. 62
Christmas punch	Vol. 25 p. 17	Crab quiche	Vol. 16 p. 88
Christmas salad	Vol. 25 p. 96	Crab soup	Vol. 21 p. 28
Chuck roast	Vol. 1 p. 38	Crab vol-au-vent	Vol. 15 p. 32
Cider (Duck breasts with)	Vol. 17 p. 46	Crabmeat casserole	Vol. 6 p. 61
Cider (Hot)	Vol. 23 p. 56	Crabmeat salad on croissants	Vol. 6 p. 64
Civet of hare	Vol. 17 p. 105	Cranberries (Leg of lamb	
Clams au gratin	Vol. 6 p. 74	glazed with)	Vol. 10 p. 76
Clams Portuguese style	Vol. 6 p. 70	Cranberry and pear sauce	Vol. 2 p. 101
Clam sauce	Vol. 11 p. 44	Cranberry bread	Vol. 19 p. 100
Clam (Spaghetti with—sauce)	Vol. 12 p. 26	Cranberry sauce	Vol. 11 p. 30
Clams (Steamed—oriental style)	Vol. 6 p. 68	Cream (Almond)	Vol. 3 p. 102
Clams (Steamed—with garlic butter)	Vol. 6 p. 66	Cream (Caramel)	Vol. 3 p. 82
Clams with risotto	Vol. 6 p. 50	Cream (Carrots with)	Vol. 13 p. 46
Classic lasagna	Vol. 12 p. 34	Cream cheese (Avocados with—	
Coconut (Apple and—Brown Betty)	Vol. 9 p. 50	and nuts)	Vol. 15 p. 78
Coconut pie	Vol. 19 p. 94	Cream cheese frosting	Vol. 3 p. 69
Coconut (Rabbit with)	Vol. 24 p. 80	Cream (Chocolate)	Vol. 3 p. 82
Coconut (Shrimps with)	Vol. 6 p. 40	Cream (Eggplant with)	Vol. 15 p. 76
Coconut tarts	Vol. 18 p. 92	Cream (Frog's legs with wine and)	Vol. 15 p. 34
Cod soup	Vol. 11 p. 78	Cream (Gnocchi with)	Vol. 12 p. 64
Cod steaks with vegetables	Vol. 5 p. 70	Cream (Linguine with mushrooms	
Codfish stew	Vol. 14 p. 90	and cream)	Vol. 12 p. 62
Coffee (Irish)	Vol. 23 p. 26	Cream (Molded—with fruit sauce)	Vol. 9 p. 60
Coffee mousse	Vol. 25 p. 90	Cream of asparagus soup	Vol. 5 p. 100
Cognac (Veal and pork terrine with)	Vol. 23 p. 74	Cream of carrot soup *chicken stock*	Vol. 12 p. 100
Cold soup	Vol. 11 p. 100	Cream of carrot soup *beef bouillon*	Vol. 25 p. 74
Coleslaw	Vol. 23 p. 20	Cream of cauliflower soup	Vol. 11 p. 66
Coleslaw (Orange)	Vol. 25 p. 82	Cream of celery soup	Vol. 6 p. 101
Compote (Apple)	Vol. 9 p. 88	Cream of cucumber and artichoke	
Compote (Fruit)	Vol. 9 p. 90	soup	Vol. 11 p. 72
Compote (Rhubarb)	Vol. 9 p. 92	Cream of leek and potato soup	Vol. 11 p. 72
Compound broths	Vol. 11 p. 82	Cream of lobster soup	Vol. 11 p. 76
Consommé Madrilène	Vol. 10 p. 101	Cream of mushroom soup	Vol. 11 p. 68
Conventional pie crust	Vol. 3 p. 84	Cream (Onions with tomatoes and)	Vol. 15 p. 80
Cookies (Almond)	Vol. 18 p. 88	Cream (Strawberry)	Vol. 3 p. 82
Cookies (Applesauce)	Vol. 9 p. 49	Cream (Tortellini with)	Vol. 12 p. 54
Cookies (Apricot)	Vol. 21 p. 98	Cream (Vanilla)	Vol. 3 p. 81
Cookies (Chocolate chip)	Vol. 3 p. 24	Cream (Veal scallopini with)	Vol. 12 p. 104
Cookies (Oatmeal)	Vol. 19 p. 98	Creamed rice with peaches	Vol. 19 p. 96
Cookies (Old fashioned raisin)	Vol. 3 p. 26	Creamy fudge	Vol. 20 p. 102
Coq au vin	Vol. 7 p. 42	Crème caramel	Vol. 9 p. 84
Coquilles Saint-Jacques	Vol. 21 p. 72	Crème royale	Vol. 6 p. 105
Corn (Beef and macaroni		Crepes (Apple)	Vol. 9 p. 99
casserole with)	Vol. 14 p. 32	Crepes (Banana)	Vol. 9 p. 88
Corn on the cob	Vol. 20 p. 36	Cross rib roast	Vol. 1 p. 32
Corn soup	Vol. 18 p. 82	Crown roast of lamb with apricots	Vol. 10 p. 72
Corn with chili sauce	Vol. 13 p. 64	Crown roast of pork	Vol. 4 p. 104
Cornish game hen (Stuffed)	Vol. 22 p. 50	Crust (Graham)	Vol. 3 p. 85
Cornish game hens with black		Cucumber and dill sauce	Vol. 11 p. 18
cherries	Vol. 7 p. 62	Cucumber and tomato soup	Vol. 21 p. 24
Cornish game hens with sausage		Cucumber (Cream of—and artichoke	
stuffing	Vol. 7 p. 64	soup)	Vol. 11 p. 72
Country omelette	Vol. 22 p. 86	Cucumber salad	Vol. 23 p. 40
Country salad	Vol. 23 p. 60	Curried apple soup	Vol. 25 p. 32
Couscous with chicken and shrimp	Vol. 2 p. 96	Curried beef	Vol. 14 p. 30
Crab Cantonese style	Vol. 6 p. 56	Curry sauce	Vol. 11 p. 30

Alphabetical Index

D

Date and bran muffins	Vol. 23 p.	66
Date squares	Vol. 3 p.	105
Deer (Leg of—*"petit maître"*)	Vol. 17 p.	80
Deer meat stew	Vol. 17 p.	86
Deer meat Swiss style	Vol. 17 p.	82
Deer meat with sweet and sour sauce	Vol. 17 p.	83
Deer (Roast leg of)	Vol. 17 p.	68
Deer steak with pepper sauce	Vol. 17 p.	84
Delicious aspic	Vol. 25 p.	22
Deviled sauce	Vol. 11 p.	32
Dill (Butter and—sauce)	Vol. 11 p.	18
Dill (Cucumber and—sauce)	Vol. 11 p.	18
Dill (Salmon with—sauce)	Vol. 21 p.	80
Dip (Lobster)	Vol. 16 p.	105
Dip (Olive)	Vol. 16 p.	105
Dip (Rosy)	Vol. 16 p.	105
Dips	Vol. 23 p.	80
Dough (Quick bread)	Vol. 9 p.	22
Dough (Sweet)	Vol. 9 p.	28
Duck breasts with cider	Vol. 17 p.	46
Duck in aspic	Vol. 18 p.	34
Duck (Oriental)	Vol. 7 p.	50
Duck Provençale	Vol. 7 p.	46
Duck (Roast—in sauce piquante)	Vol. 7 p.	48
Duck (Roast—stuffed with oysters)	Vol. 17 p.	52
Duck (Roast—with orange sauce)	Vol. 2 p.	44
Duck with apples	Vol. 17 p.	48
Duck with olives	Vol. 7 p.	53
Dumplings (Chicken with)	Vol. 2 p.	60

E

Egg and lemon soup	Vol. 24 p. 36
Egg and salmon loaf	Vol. 23 p. 34
Egg (Ham and)	Vol. 20 p. 64
Egg (Ham and—terrine)	Vol. 23 p. 42
Egg ramekins	Vol. 23 p. 61
Egg (Scrambled—tartlets)	Vol. 16 p. 64
Egg surprise	Vol. 23 p. 24
Eggplant and tomato fricassee	Vol. 15 p. 64
Eggplant parmesan	Vol. 16 p. 72
Eggplant ragoût with lobster tails	Vol. 15 p. 36
Eggplant (Spaghettini with)	Vol. 14 p. 96
Eggplant with cream	Vol. 15 p. 76
Eggs (Antilles)	Vol. 25 p. 54
Eggs Benedict	Vol. 16 p. 42
Eggs en matelote	Vol. 16 p. 48
Eggs (Fried rice with ham and)	Vol. 18 p. 78
Eggs in ramekins	Vol. 16 p. 54
Eggs jardinière	Vol. 16 p. 46
Eggs on a muffin	Vol. 23 p. 81
Eggs poached in tomato sauce	Vol. 16 p. 45
Eggs (Poached—on asparagus mousse)	Vol. 23 p. 40
Eggs (Scrambled—with rice)	Vol. 16 p. 53
Eggs (Scrambled—with smoked salmon)	Vol. 16 p. 50
Eggs (Tomatoes stuffed with)	Vol. 16 p. 61
Emincé of veal with cream sauce	Vol. 25 p. 76
Endive and ham roll-ups	Vol. 23 p. 90
Endive au gratin	Vol. 16 p. 78
Escargots with garlic and green onion	Vol. 6 p. 84
Espagnole sauce	Vol. 11 p. 22

F

Fennel sauce	Vol. 11 p. **48**
Festive fruit punch	Vol. 23 p. **76**
Festive pudding	Vol. 23 p. **96**
Festive summer vegetables	Vol. 15 p. **66**
Feta cheese (Shrimp with—in tomato sauce)	Vol. 19 p. **82**
Fettuccine Alfredo	Vol. 7 p. **100**
Fettuccine verde	Vol. 2 p. **92**
Fettuccine with red wine	Vol. 12 p. **45**
Fettuccine with Roquefort cheese	Vol. 12 p. **46**
Fettuccine with seafood	Vol. 6 p. **83**
Fiddleheads	Vol. 25 p. **49**
Filet mignon	Vol. 1 p. **51**
Fillet of sole Creole style	Vol. 22 p. **74**
Fillets of sole breaded Italian style	Vol. 5 p. **46**
Fillets of sole with almonds	Vol. 5 p. **45**
Fish and fruit kebabs	Vol. 5 p. **58**
Fish and leek soup	Vol. 11 p. **78**
Fish and zucchini chowder	Vol. 5 p. **56**
Fish croquettes with shrimp sauce	Vol. 5 p. **92**
Fish (Grilled—with coriander)	Vol. 24 p. **60**
Fish stock	Vol. 11 p. **59**
Fish stock sauce	Vol. 16 p. **58**
Fisherman's soup	Vol. 19 p. **28**
Fisherman's stew	Vol. 19 p. **80**
Flamboyant punch	Vol. 25 p. **15**
Flan (Apricot)	Vol. 10 p. **105**
Flan (Cheese and tomato)	Vol. 16 p. **92**
Flan (Fruit—with pastry cream)	Vol. 3 p. **98**
Flan (Leek)	Vol. 13 p. **94**
Flan (Pineapple)	Vol. 9 p. **56**
Fondue (Chocolate)	Vol. 3 p. **102**
Fondue (Swiss)	Vol. 16 p. **66**
Frankfurters and beans	Vol. 8 p. **96**
Frankfurters (Spicy)	Vol. 15 p. **45**
French-Canadian tourtière	Vol. 4 p. **86**
Fricassee (Chicken)	Vol. 7 p. **90**
Fricassee (Eggplant and tomato)	Vol. 15 p. **64**
Fricassee (Lobster)	Vol. 23 p. **94**
Fricassee (Sausage)	Vol. 4 p. **90**
Fricassee (Veal)	Vol. 10 p. **54**
Fried rice with ham and eggs	Vol. 18 p. **78**
Fried rice with shrimp	Vol. 12 p. **70**
Fried rice with soy sauce	Vol. 18 p. **74**
Fried vegetables Chinese style	Vol. 13 p. **88**
Frogs' legs Provençale	Vol. 6 p. **72**
Frogs' legs with wine and cream	Vol. 15 p. **34**
Frosting (Chocolate)	Vol. 3 p. **69**
Frosting cream cheese	Vol. 3 p. **69**
Frosting (Japanese)	Vol. 3 p. **68**
Frosting (Mocha)	Vol. 3 p. **68**
Fruit and pecan tart	Vol. 13 p. **105**
Fruit cake	Vol. 3 p. **56**
Fruit compote	Vol. 9 p. **90**
Fruit cup with Grand Marnier	Vol. 25 p. **38**
Fruit (Festive—punch)	Vol. 23 p. **76**
Fruit-filled pineapple	Vol. 22 p. **105**
Fruit (Fish and—kebabs)	Vol. 5 p. **58**
Fruit flan with pastry cream	Vol. 3 p. **98**
Fruit gratin	Vol. 9 p. **57**
Fruit (Hot—kebabs)	Vol. 23 p. **87**
Fruit (Hot—punch)	Vol. 20 p. **76**
Fruit (Hot—salad)	Vol. 23 p. **105**
Fruit omelette	Vol. 16 p. **40**
Fruit pizza	Vol. 25 p. **50**
Fruit punch	Vol. 23 p. **86**
Fruit punch *with white wine*	Vol. 25 p. **16**
Fruit salad	Vol. 8 p. **105**
Fruit salad *fruit and canteloupe*	Vol. 23 p. **67**
Fruit tart	Vol. 21 p. **92**
Fruit (Veal with stewed)	Vol. 10 p. **38**
Fudge (Chocolate)	Vol. 20 p. **94**
Fudge (Creamy)	Vol. 20 p. **102**

Garden vegetables with vinaigrette
   dressing   Vol. 7 p. **101**
Garlic bread   Vol. 22 p. **28**
Garlic butter   Vol. 1 p. **55**
Garlic butter (Prawns with)   Vol. 6 p. **42**
Garlic butter (Shrimps with)   Vol. 6 p. **34**
Garlic butter (Steamed clams with) Vol. 6 p. **66**
Garlic chicken   Vol. 23 p. **64**
Garlic (Chicken with)   Vol. 7 p. **66**
Garlic (Escargots with—and green
   onion)   Vol. 6 p. **84**

Garlic (Potatoes with a—stuffing) Vol. 15 p. **103**
Garlic (Spaghettini with)   Vol. 12 p. **30**
Garlic (Zucchini with)   Vol. 25 p. **89**
Garnish (Green pea)   Vol. 16 p. **60**
Garnish (Mushroom)   Vol. 16 p. **60**
Garnish (Spinach)   Vol. 16 p. **60**
Gazpacho soup   Vol. 11 p. **102**
German chocolate cake   Vol. 9 p. **36**
Ginger (Mandarin and—sorbet)   Vol. 9 p. **62**
Ginger (Chicken with)   Vol. 2 p. **80**
Gingerbread men   Vol. 25 p. **105**
Glazed baked ham   Vol. 4 p. **38**
Glazed carrots   Vol. 13 p. **45**
Glazed carrots *with honey and*
   ginger   Vol. 20 p. **32**
Glazed ham with peaches   Vol. 11 p. **53**
Glazed lamb shoulder   Vol. 25 p. **86**
Glazed pears   Vol. 21 p. **90**
Glazed pork roast   Vol. 4 p. **24**
Glazed vegetables   Vol. 25 p. **103**
Gnocchi with cheese and tomato
   sauce   Vol. 15 p. **84**

H

Gnocchi with cream	Vol. 12 p. 64
Golden pork chops	Vol. 4 p. 50
Golden punch	Vol. 25 p. 15
Goose French style	Vol. 7 p. 36
Goose stew	Vol. 17 p. 62
Goose with apples	Vol. 17 p. 60
Goose with cream sauce	Vol. 17 p. 64
Goose with pears in brandy	Vol. 7 p. 34
Graham crust	Vol. 3 p. 85
Grandmother's macaroni	Vol. 8 p. 86
Granola balls	Vol. 20 p. 90
Grape mousse	Vol. 9 p. 82
Grapefruit with rum	Vol. 23 p. 51
Grapes (Pickerel stuffed with green—and almonds	Vol. 5 p. 50
Grapes (Quails with green)	Vol. 2 p. 46
Green beans with tomato sauce	Vol. 13 p. 62
Green cherries (Quick bread ring with nuts and)	Vol. 9 p. 23
Green onion (Escargots with garlic and)	Vol. 6 p. 84
Green pea garnish	Vol. 16 p. 60
Green salad	Vol. 25 p. 42
Green salad with herbs *and Boston lettuce*	Vol. 23 p. 50
Green salad *with Romaine lettuce*	Vol. 13 p. 104
Grilled fish with coriander	Vol. 24 p. 60
Ground beef base	Vol. 1 p. 90
Ground beef stew	Vol. 8 p. 56
Ground beef casserole *with potatoes and carrots*	Vol. 22 p. 40
Ground beef casserole *with green beans*	Vol. 1 p. 72
Ground pork with broccoli	Vol. 18 p. 48
Gruyère (Apples with—cheese)	Vol. 23 p. 27
Guinea fowl with raspberries	Vol. 7 p. 104
Haddock fillets with mushroom sauce	Vol. 22 p. 68
Haddock (Norway—fillets on a bed of spinach	Vol. 5 p. 64
Haddock (Norway—with herb sauce)	Vol. 5 p. 62
Haddock (Pilaf of)	Vol. 21 p. 76
Haddock poached in milk	Vol. 5 p. 61
Haddock (Smoked)	Vol. 24 p. 56
Halibut fillets with broccoli	Vol. 5 p. 86
Halibut steaks	Vol. 22 p. 70
Halibut steaks in lettuce leaves	Vol. 5 p. 88
Ham and egg	Vol. 20 p. 64
Ham and egg terrine	Vol. 23 p. 42
Ham and macaroni casserole	Vol. 14 p. 95
Ham and noodles au gratin	Vol. 4 p. 40
Ham and watercress soup	Vol. 11 p. 84
Ham (Broccoli and—casserole)	Vol. 13 p. 56
Ham (Broccoli and—rolls)	Vol. 25 p. 44
Ham (Canadian)	Vol. 4 p. 40
Ham (Chicken,—and rice soup)	Vol. 24 p. 83
Ham (Chicken and—soup)	Vol. 11 p. 84
Ham (Endive and—roll-ups)	Vol. 23 p. 90
Ham (Fried rice with—and eggs)	Vol. 18 p. 78
Ham (Glazed baked)	Vol. 4 p. 38
Ham glazed with orange	Vol. 22 p. 61
Ham (Glazed—with peaches)	Vol. 11 p. 53
Ham (Hot—sandwich)	Vol. 14 p. 100
Ham in beer	Vol. 23 p. 22
Ham loaf	Vol. 4 p. 36
Ham (Maple)	Vol. 23 p. 52
Ham meatballs	Vol. 4 p. 46
Ham meatballs *with pineapple rings*	Vol. 21 p. 68
Ham mousse *with Madeira wine*	Vol. 15 p. 92
Ham mousse *with pecans and celery*	Vol. 23 p. 102
Ham parmentier	Vol. 4 p. 45
Ham rolls	Vol. 15 p. 48
Ham steak and pineapple	Vol. 4 p. 32
Ham (Veal breast stuffed with spinach and)	Vol. 10 p. 104
Ham vol-au-vent	Vol. 4 p. 48

I-J

Ham (Squid stuffed with)	Vol. 6 p.	86
Ham steak and pineapple	Vol. 4 p.	32
Ham (Veal breast stuffed with spinach and)	Vol. 10 p.	104
Ham vol-au-vent	Vol. 4 p.	48
Ham with maple syrup	Vol. 4 p.	34
Hamburger quiche	Vol. 8 p.	90
Hamburgers	Vol. 1 p.	78
Hare casserole	Vol. 17 p.	98
Hare (Civet of)	Vol. 17 p.	105
Hare hunter style	Vol. 17 p.	101
Hare with beer	Vol. 17 p.	100
Harvard beets	Vol. 19 p.	48
Headcheese	Vol. 15 p.	96
Herring (Marinated salt)	Vol. 5 p.	94
Herring Oslo style	Vol. 24 p.	88
Holiday turkey	Vol. 25 p.	24
Hollandaise Chantilly sauce	Vol. 11 p.	36
Hollandaise sauce	Vol. 11 p.	12
Homemade pork rillettes	Vol. 4 p.	82
Home-style soup	Vol. 11 p.	98
Honey-glazed chicken	Vol. 18 p.	24
Honey (Pineapple and—ring)	Vol. 9 p.	24
Honey (Whole wheat—muffins)	Vol. 3 p.	43
Hors d'oeuvres (Seafood)	Vol. 6 p.	92
Horseradish sauce	Vol. 11 p.	24
Hot chicken sandwich	Vol. 7 p.	86
Hot chocolate	Vol. 23 p.	86
Hot cider	Vol. 23 p.	56
Hot cross buns	Vol. 9 p.	30
Hot fruit kebabs	Vol. 23 p.	87
Hot fruit punch	Vol. 20 p.	76
Hot fruit salad	Vol. 23 p.	105
Hot ham sandwich	Vol. 14 p.	100
Hot'n spicy pork chops	Vol. 4 p.	62
Hot snack	Vol. 16 p.	100
Hunter's stew	Vol. 24 p.	46
Hzing Zen jelly	Vol. 18 p.	86
Iced melons	Vol. 23 p.	77
Indian rice	Vol. 12 p.	86
Individual cheesecakes	Vol. 22 p.	94
Irish coffee	Vol. 23 p.	26
Italian meat loaf	Vol. 8 p.	82
Italian sauce	Vol. 1 p.	88
Italian sauce *with meat*	Vol. 11 p.	50
Italian vegetable sauce	Vol. 16 p.	59
Jam (Blueberry)	Vol. 9 p.	95
Jam (Cherry)	Vol. 9 p.	97
Jam (Raspberry)	Vol. 9 p.	96
Jam (Strawberry)	Vol. 9 p.	94
Japanese frosting	Vol. 3 p.	68
Japanese punch	Vol. 25 p.	17
Jelly (Hzing Zen)	Vol. 18 p.	86
Jujube cake	Vol. 25 p.	18
Julienne of veal with rice	Vol. 14 p.	82
Julienne (Vegetables)	Vol. 23 p.	80

K-L

Ketchup (Tomato) — Vol. 13 p. 74

Lamb chops (Braised—with vegetables) — Vol. 10 p. 82
Lamb chops English style — Vol. 22 p. 78
Lamb chops Italian style — Vol. 10 p. 59
Lamb chops with apples — Vol. 10 p. 78
Lamb chops with beans — Vol. 19 p. 70
Lamb chops with orange sauce — Vol. 10 p. 70
Lamb chops with parsley — Vol. 14 p. 86
Lamb (Crown roast of—with apricots) — Vol. 10 p. 72
Lamb (Glazed—shoulder) — Vol. 25 p. 86
Lamb liver (Braised) — Vol. 10 p. 92
Lamb kebabs — Vol. 10 p. 90
Lamb (Leg of—glazed with cranberries) — Vol. 10 p. 76
Lamb (Leg of—with rosemary) — Vol. 10 p. 74
Lamb meat loaf — Vol. 22 p. 82
Lamb meatballs — Vol. 10 p. 94
Lamb (Pita sandwiches with—meatballs) — Vol. 21 p. 70
Lamb (Rack of—French style) — Vol. 10 p. 88
Lamb (Ragoût of) — Vol. 10 p. 96
Lamb (Roast—with Madeira) — Vol. 10 p. 84
Lamb (Shank of—European style) — Vol. 10 p. 80
Lamb stew — Vol. 10 p. 83
Lasagna — Vol. 8 p. 88
Lasagna (Classic) — Vol. 12 p. 34
Lasagna (Spinach—Bolognese) — Vol. 12 p. 36
Lasagna with four cheeses — Vol. 12 p. 38
Lasagna with salmon — Vol. 12 p. 40
Lazy pudding — Vol. 3 p. 78
Leek (Cream of—and broccoli soup) — Vol. 21 p. 36
Leek (Cream of—and potato soup) — Vol. 11 p. 72
Leek (Chicken and—pie) — Vol. 23 p. 54
Leek (Fish and—soup) — Vol. 11 p. 78
Leek flan — Vol. 13 p. 94
Leek soup — Vol. 1 p. 100
Leeks (Mackerel with) — Vol. 5 p. 66
Leeks (Marinated) — Vol. 15 p. 100

Leeks on a bed of noodles — Vol. 15 p. 82
Leeks (Pork with) — Vol. 14 p. 40
Leg of deer "petit maître" — Vol. 17 p. 80
Leg of lamb glazed with cranberries — Vol. 10 p. 76
Leg of lamb with rosemary — Vol. 10 p. 74
Lemon butter (Burbot with) — Vol. 5 p. 83
Lemon butter sauce — Vol. 11 p. 36
Lemon chicken — Vol. 2 p. 64
Lemon chicken with parsley — Vol. 2 p. 78
Lemon (Egg and—soup) — Vol. 24 p. 36
Lemon meringue pie — Vol. 3 p. 94
Lemon (Red mullet with—and chives) — Vol. 24 p. 50
Lemon rice — Vol. 12 p. 82
Lemon sauce — Vol. 11 p. 20
Lemon (Scallops with—and spinach) — Vol. 19 p. 78
Lemon topping — Vol. 3 p. 73
Lentil and ground beef casserole — Vol. 21 p. 64
Lentil and tomato soup — Vol. 19 p. 32
Lentil soup — Vol. 11 p. 92
Lentil soup with red lentils and potatoes — Vol. 13 p. 100
Lettuce (Boston—with tarragon vinegar) — Vol. 23 p. 100
Lettuce (Halibut steaks in—leaves) — Vol. 5 p. 88
Lettuce leaves stuffed with pork — Vol. 18 p. 42
Lichee mousse — Vol. 18 p. 90
Lichee sauce — Vol. 18 p. 70
Lime (Strawberry-—chiffon cake) — Vol. 23 p. 36
Linguine with mushrooms and cream — Vol. 12 p. 62
Linguine with shrimps and tomatoes — Vol. 21 p. 82
Liver loaf — Vol. 21 p. 45
Lobster dip — Vol. 16 p. 105
Lobster (Cream of—soup) — Vol. 11 p. 76
Lobster (Eggplant ragoût with—tails) — Vol. 15 p. 36
Lobster fricassee — Vol. 23 p. 94
Lobster meat au gratin — Vol. 6 p. 28
Lobster (Rice and—salad) — Vol. 12 p. 84
Lobster (Stuffed—tails) — Vol. 6 p. 30
Lobster Thermidor — Vol. 6 p. 24
Lobster with mushrooms — Vol. 18 p. 54
Lotus root salad — Vol. 18 p. 96

M

Macaroni and cheese	Vol. 16 p. 82
Macaroni (Beef and—casserole with corn)	Vol. 14 p. 32
Macaroni casserole	Vol. 23 p. 82
Macaroni (Grandmother's)	Vol. 8 p. 86
Macaroni (Ham and—casserole)	Vol. 14 p. 95
Macaroni salad	Vol. 23 p. 30
Macaroni stir-fry	Vol. 1 p. 92
Macaroni with cheddar cheese	Vol. 12 p. 61
Macédoine of beef	Vol. 1 p. 45
Macédoine of vegetables with cheese	Vol. 16 p. 74
Mackerel fillets with sweet and sour sauce	Vol. 5 p. 68
Mackerel with leeks	Vol. 5 p. 66
Madeira sauce	Vol. 11 p. 32
Mandarin and ginger sorbet	Vol. 9 p. 62
Mandarin cheesecake	Vol. 9 p. 40
Mandarin (Oriental beef with)	Vol. 8 p. 50
Manicotti (Salmon)	Vol. 5 p. 34
Manicotti with pike	Vol. 12 p. 53
Manicotti with spinach	Vol. 19 p. 84
Maple cream pie	Vol. 3 p. 92
Maple ham	Vol. 23 p. 52
Maple pie	Vol. 23 p. 56
Maple syrup	Vol. 4 p. 34
Maple syrup (Pears with)	Vol. 9 p. 54
Mariana sauce	Vol. 11 p. 43
Marinades for game	Vol. 17 p. 56
Marinated chicken kebabs	Vol. 2 p. 70
Marinated leeks	Vol. 15 p. 100
Marinated pork tenderloin with rice	Vol. 18 p. 38
Marinated salt herring	Vol. 5 p. 94
Marinated steak	Vol. 8 p. 72
Marinated turkey cutlets	Vol. 7 p. 28
Marinated vegetables	Vol. 25 p. 59
Marshmallow squares	Vol. 20 p. 86
Meat loaf (Caribou)	Vol. 17 p. 90
Meat loaf (Italian)	Vol. 8 p. 82
Meat loaf (Lamb)	Vol. 22 p. 82
Meat loaf (Moose)	Vol. 17 p. 72
Meat loaf (Old-fashioned)	Vol. 8 p. 66
Meat loaf with barbecue flavor	Vol. 8 p. 68
Meat loaf with chili sauce	Vol. 1 p. 84
Meat loaf with pistachios	Vol. 24 p. 62
Meat loaf with spinach	Vol. 1 p. 80
Meat loaf with sweet and sour sauce	Vol. 1 p. 83
Meat loaves	Vol. 1 p. 82
Meat stock	Vol. 11 p. 58
Meatball kebabs	Vol. 8 p. 58
Meatballs	Vol. 1 p. 86
Meatballs (Ham)	Vol. 4 p. 46
Meatballs (Ham) with pineapple rings	Vol. 21 p. 68
Meatballs (Lamb)	Vol. 10 p. 94
Meatballs (Moose—with cream sauce)	Vol. 17 p. 76
Meatballs (Pita sandwiches with lamb)	Vol. 21 p. 70
Meatballs (Poached—with lemon sauce)	Vol. 24 p. 42
Meatballs (Pork)	Vol. 18 p. 46
Meatballs (Sausage)	Vol. 14 p. 80
Meatballs (Spaghetti with—and tomato sauce)	Vol. 12 p. 22
Meatballs with baked beans	Vol. 8 p. 61
Medallions of pork with Bordelaise sauce	Vol. 4 p. 76
Medallions of pork with fennel	Vol. 4 p. 78
Mediterranean medley	Vol. 15 p. 88
Melon (Winter—soup)	Vol. 18 p. 96
Melons (Iced)	Vol. 23 p. 77
Mexican beef	Vol. 8 p. 84
Mexican beef stew	Vol. 19 p. 66
Mexican-style pita sandwich	Vol. 19 p. 72
Milk (Haddock poached in)	Vol. 5 p. 61
Minestrone soup beef stock	Vol. 11 p. 96
Minestrone soup chicken bouillon	Vol. 21 p. 34
Mini chicken kebabs	Vol. 15 p. 46
Mini pizza Italian style	Vol. 14 p. 102
Mini pizza Neapolitan style	Vol. 14 p. 101
Mini-pizza	Vol. 16 p. 98
Mint parfait	Vol. 7 p. 105
Mint tea	Vol. 23 p. 76
Mixed vegetables broccoli, carrots, cauliflower	Vol. 13 p. 50
Mixed vegetables rutabagas, leeks, peppers	Vol. 25 p. 69

Alphabetical Index

Mocha cake	Vol. 25 p. 105
Mocha frosting	Vol. 3 p. 68
Molasses bran muffins	Vol. 3 p. 44
Molded cream with fruit sauce	Vol. 9 p. 60
Monday omelette	Vol. 16 p. 32
Moose meat loaf	Vol. 17 p. 72
Moose meat with mushrooms	Vol. 17 p. 74
Moose meatballs with cream sauce	Vol. 17 p. 76
Moose (Roast)	Vol. 17 p. 68
Moose stew	Vol. 17 p. 70
Mornay sauce	Vol. 11 p. 14
Moussaka	Vol. 8 p. 62
Mousse (Bourbon)	Vol. 25 p. 70
Mousse (Cherry)	Vol. 9 p. 80
Mousse (Chestnut)	Vol. 12 p. 105
Mousse (Chocolate)	Vol. 3 p. 101
Mousse (Chocolate mint)	Vol. 9 p. 78
Mousse (Coffee)	Vol. 25 p. 90
Mousse (Grape)	Vol. 9 p. 82
Mousse (Ham)	Vol. 15 p. 92
Mousse (Lichee)	Vol. 18 p. 90
Mousse (Peach halves with shrimp)	Vol. 22 p. 100
Mousse (Poached eggs on asparagus)	Vol. 23 p. 40
Mousse (Salmon)	Vol. 22 p. 26
Mousse (Sole)	Vol. 25 p. 94
Mousse (Strawberry)	Vol. 3 p. 102
Mousse (Tomato)	Vol. 13 p. 82
Muffin (Eggs on a)	Vol. 23 p. 81
Muffins (Bran—with molasses)	Vol. 23 p. 76
Muffins (Cheese)	Vol. 19 p. 88
Muffins (Chocolate)	Vol. 3 p. 42
Muffins (Date and bran)	Vol. 23 p. 66
Muffins (Molasses bran)	Vol. 3 p. 44
Muffins (Orange)	Vol. 21 p. 86
Muffins (Wheat germ)	Vol. 21 p. 88
Muffins (Whole wheat honey)	Vol. 3 p. 43
Mulled wine	Vol. 25 p. 16
Mullet (Red—*en papillote*)	Vol. 5 p. 90
Mullet (Red—with lemon and chives)	Vol. 24 p. 50
Mushroom and cauliflower salad	Vol. 22 p. 101
Mushroom (Artichoke and—salad)	Vol. 13 p. 86
Mushroom (Brown rice and—salad)	Vol. 12 p. 101
Mushroom (Cream of—soup)	Vol. 11 p. 68
Mushroom garnish	Vol. 16 p. 60
Mushroom (Haddock fillets with—sauce)	Vol. 22 p. 68
Mushroom (Stuffed—caps)	Vol. 23 p. 100
Mushroom (Stuffed—caps) *with celery*	Vol. 21 p. 50
Mushrooms (Brussels sprouts with)	Vol. 13 p. 59
Mushrooms Greek style	Vol. 15 p. 101
Mushrooms (Linguine with—and cream)	Vol. 12 p. 62
Mushrooms (Lobster with)	Vol. 18 p. 54
Mushrooms (Moose meat with)	Vol. 17 p. 74
Mushrooms (Oysters sautéed with)	Vol. 6 p. 78
Mushrooms (Veal escallops with— and wine	Vol. 19 p. 64
Mussels Bordelaise	Vol. 25 p. 64
Mussels Marinière	Vol. 5 p. 101
Mustard (Rabbit with)	Vol. 25 p. 56
Mustard (Roast beef with—sauce)	Vol. 23 p. 72
Mustard sauce	Vol. 11 p. 22

Alphabetical Index

N

Neapolitan pork chops	Vol. 4 p.	**64**
New England braised beef	Vol. 8 p.	**28**
New England stew	Vol. 24 p.	**94**
Newburg sauce	Vol. 11 p.	**24**
Noodle (Chicken—soup)	Vol. 11 p.	**90**
Noodle (Tomato and—soup)	Vol. 11 p.	**88**
Noodle (Vegetable and—soup)	Vol. 20 p.	**24**
Noodles (Chicken livers with)	Vol. 2 p.	**68**
Noodles (Ham and—au gratin)	Vol. 4 p.	**40**
Noodles (Leeks on a bed of)	Vol. 15 p.	**82**
Noodles (Rice with)	Vol. 20 p.	**40**
Noodles (Tuna and)	Vol. 14 p.	**94**
Norway haddock fillets on a bed of spinach	Vol. 5 p.	**64**
Norway haddock with herb sauce	Vol. 5 p.	**62**
Nuts (Avocados with cream cheese and)	Vol. 15 p.	**78**
Nuts (Chicken stuffed with celery and)	Vol. 2 p.	**50**
Nuts (Quick bread ring with—and green cherries)	Vol. 9 p.	**23**

Oatmeal cookies	Vol. 19 **p.**	**98**
Old-fashioned meat loaf	Vol. 8 **p.**	**66**
Old-fashioned raisin cookies	Vol. 3 **p.**	**26**
Olive dip	Vol. 16 **p.**	**105**
Olives (Beef with)	Vol. 1 **p.**	**68**
Olives (Duck with)	Vol. 7 **p.**	**53**

Omelette (Apple)	Vol. 20 **p.**	**98**
Omelette (Apple—flambé)	Vol. 16 **p.**	**38**
Omelette (Chicken)	Vol. 2 **p.**	**88**
Omelette (Country)	Vol. 22 **p.**	**86**
Omelette country style	Vol. 16 **p.**	**24**
Omelette (Fruit)	Vol. 16 **p.**	**40**
Omelette (Monday)	Vol. 16 **p.**	**32**
Omelette parmentier	Vol. 16 **p.**	**62**
Omelette Provençale	Vol. 16 **p.**	**26**
Omelette (Salmon)	Vol. 16 **p.**	**36**
Omelette (Spanish)	Vol. 16 **p.**	**34**
Omelette (Springtime)	Vol. 16 **p.**	**30**
Omelette (Tuna)	Vol. 5 **p.**	**74**
Omelette with tomato sauce	Vol. 23 **p.**	**92**
Omelette (Zucchini)	Vol. 16 **p.**	**28**
Onion and tomato casserole	Vol. 13 **p.**	**78**
Onion (Broccoli and—soup)	Vol. 19 **p.**	**30**

P

Onion (Quails with)	Vol. 7 p. 54
Onion soup au gratin	Vol. 11 p. 94
Onions (Pork and)	Vol. 14 p. 38
Onions (Potatoes with)	Vol. 13 p. 40
Onions (Stuffed)	Vol. 13 p. 92
Onions with tomatoes and cream	Vol. 15 p. 80
Orange (Beef sauté with—segments)	Vol. 19 p. 68
Orange (Beef with)	Vol. 22 p. 34
Orange Charlotte	Vol. 23 p. 57
Orange (Chicken with)	Vol. 2 p. 66
Orange coleslaw	Vol. 25 p. 82
Orange crown cake	Vol. 25 p. 60
Orange (Ham glazed with)	Vol. 22 p. 61
Orange muffins	Vol. 21 p. 86
Orange (Rice and—stuffing)	Vol. 12 p. 80
Oranges in wine	Vol. 21 p. 96
Oriental beef with mandarins	Vol. 8 p. 50
Oriental chicken	Vol. 22 p. 46
Oriental duck	Vol. 7 p. 50
Oriental turkey	Vol. 2 p. 73
Osso Bucco	Vol. 24 p. 26
Oyster (Chinese vegetables with—sauce)	Vol. 18 p. 62
Oyster soup	Vol. 11 p. 80
Oysters au gratin	Vol. 6 p. 54
Oysters (Roast duck stuffed with)	Vol. 17 p. 52
Oysters sautéed with mushrooms	Vol. 6 p. 78

Paella	Vol. 6 p. 96
Paella (Vegetable)	Vol. 21 p. 61
Parfait (Mint)	Vol. 7 p. 105
Parmesan sauce	Vol. 11 p. 22
Parmesan white sauce	Vol. 16 p. 58
Parsley potatoes	Vol. 13 p. 28
Parsnip (Potato and—gratin)	Vol. 25 p. 101
Partridge (Baked beans with)	Vol. 17 p. 36
Partridge with cabbage	Vol. 17 p. 34
Partridge with red wine	Vol. 17 p. 28
Partridge with sauerkraut	Vol. 17 p. 32
Partridge with truffles	Vol. 17 p. 30
Pasta filled with a surprise	Vol. 12 p. 48
Pastry cream	Vol. 3 p. 100
Pâté (Chicken liver and pork)	Vol. 15 p. 94
Pâté (Pork)	Vol. 22 p. 24
Pâté (Pork) *with bacon and pork liver*	Vol. 4 p. 74
Pâté (Shrimp)	Vol. 25 p. 102
Paupiettes (Chicken)	Vol. 22 p. 48
Paupiettes of veal	Vol. 10 p. 40
Pea (Purée of—soup)	Vol. 11 p. 67
Pea soup	Vol. 11 p. 96
Peach halves with shrimp mousse	Vol. 22 p. 100
Peach pie	Vol. 3 p. 91
Peaches (Chicken breasts with)	Vol. 7 p. 82
Peaches (Creamed rice with)	Vol. 19 p. 96
Peaches (Glazed ham with)	Vol. 11 p. 53
Peaches (Stewed—and plums)	Vol. 23 p. 86
Peaches stuffed with almonds and raisins	Vol. 19 p. 92
Peanut butter cake	Vol. 9 p. 38
Peanuts (Chicken with)	Vol. 18 p. 28
Pear and watercress soup	Vol. 11 p. 102
Pear (Cranberry and—sauce)	Vol. 2 p. 101
Pears Alma	Vol. 9 p. 53
Pears (Glazed)	Vol. 21 p. 90
Pears (Goose with—in brandy)	Vol. 7 p. 34
Pears in red wine	Vol. 9 p. 52
Pears (Poached—with raspberry coulis)	Vol. 5 p. 105
Pears with maple syrup	Vol. 9 p. 54
Peas (Casserole of artichokes and)	Vol. 13 p. 83

Peas (Quail casserole with)	Vol. 7 p. 61
Pecan (Fruit and—tart)	Vol. 13 p. 105
Pecan pie	Vol. 3 p. 93
Pepper (Rutabaga and green—with cheese)	Vol. 13 p. 53
Pepper steak	Vol. 8 p. 32
Pepper (Stuffed—canapés)	Vol. 13 p. 80
Peppercorn sauce	Vol. 11 p. 48
Peppers (Beef and)	Vol. 18 p. 100
Peppers (Beef with red)	Vol. 8 p. 48
Peppers (Beef with sliced)	Vol. 8 p. 78
Peppers (Pork with red)	Vol. 14 p. 44
Peppers (Stuffed)	Vol. 1 p. 95
Perch with tomatoes	Vol. 5 p. 72
Perch (Yellow—with beer)	Vol. 5 p. 84
Pesto	Vol. 11 p. 44
Pheasant Basque style	Vol. 17 p. 40
Pheasant (Burgundy)	Vol. 17 p. 38
Pheasant royale	Vol. 17 p. 42
Pickerel fillets sautéed in butter	Vol. 5 p. 53
Pickerel stuffed with green grapes and almonds	Vol. 5 p. 50
Pie (Apple)	Vol. 17 p. 104
Pie (Blueberry)	Vol. 24 p. 105
Pie (Cheesy beef)	Vol. 8 p. 64
Pie (Chicken and leek)	Vol. 23 p. 54
Pie (Coconut)	Vol. 19 p. 94
Pie crust (Conventional)	Vol. 3 p. 84
Pie (Lemon meringue)	Vol. 3 p. 94
Pie (Maple)	Vol. 23 p. 56
Pie (Maple cream)	Vol. 3 p. 92
Pie (Peach)	Vol. 3 p. 91
Pie (Pecan)	Vol. 3 p. 93
Pie (Pumpkin)	Vol. 25 p. 79
Pie (Salmon)	Vol. 5 p. 30
Pie (Shepherd's)	Vol. 1 p. 93
Pie (Strawberry)	Vol. 3 p. 90
Pie (Sugar)	Vol. 3 p. 88
Pies (Chicken)	Vol. 7 p. 88
Pigs' trotters stew	Vol. 25 p. 98
Pigs' trotters stew *Quebec*	Vol. 24 p. 102
Pike (Manicotti with)	Vol. 12 p. 53
Pike (Sea—in caper sauce)	Vol. 5 p. 96
Pilaf of haddock	Vol. 21 p. 76
Pineapple and honey ring	Vol. 9 p. 24
Pineapple and strawberry punch	Vol. 23 p. 97
Pineapple cake	Vol. 3 p. 52
Pineapple (Chicken with)	Vol. 18 p. 32
Pineapple flan	Vol. 9 p. 56
Pineapple (Fruit-filled)	Vol. 22 p. 105
Pineapple fruit salad	Vol. 9 p. 58
Pineapple (Ham steak and)	Vol. 4 p. 32
Pineapple (Lemon and—pudding)	Vol. 9 p. 71
Pineapple (Navy beans with)	Vol. 21 p. 46
Pineapple salad	Vol. 23 p. 46
Pistachios (Chicken breasts with)	Vol. 7 p. 68
Pistachios (Meat loaf with)	Vol. 24 p. 62
Pita bread snack-Greek style	Vol. 14 p. 36
Pita (Mexican-style—sandwich)	Vol. 19 p. 72
Pita sandwiches with lamb meatballs	Vol. 21 p. 70
Pizza (Mini-)	Vol. 16 p. 98
Pizza (Mini—Italian style)	Vol. 14 p. 102
Pizza (Mini—Neapolitan style)	Vol. 14 p. 101
Pizza soufflé	Vol. 16 p. 90
Pizza with shrimp	Vol. 14 p. 105
Pizzas	Vol. 20 p. 48

Pizzas (Mini)	Vol. 20 **p.** 82
Plum pudding	Vol. 24 **p.** 54
Plum sauce	Vol. 18 **p.** 68
Plums (Stewed peaches and)	Vol. 23 **p.** 86
Poached eggs on asparagus mousse	Vol. 23 **p.** 40
Poached meatballs with lemon sauce	Vol. 24 **p.** 42
Poached pears with raspberry coulis	Vol. 5 **p.** 105
Polonaise sauce	Vol. 11 **p.** 38
Poppy seed bread	Vol. 3 **p.** 33
Pork (All purpose—base)	Vol. 4 **p.** 92
Pork and onions	Vol. 14 **p.** 38
Pork and potatoes with sweet sauce	Vol. 24 **p.** 78
Pork (Chicken liver and—pâté)	Vol. 15 **p.** 94
Pork Chop Suey	Vol. 18 **p.** 53
Pork (Chop Suey with)	Vol. 4 **p.** 96
Pork chops en papillotes	Vol. 4 **p.** 56
Pork chops Normandy style	Vol. 4 **p.** 58
Pork chops on macaroni	Vol. 4 **p.** 70
Pork chops with a julienne garnish	Vol. 4 **p.** 54
Pork chops with fine herbs	Vol. 22 **p.** 64
Pork chops with prunes	Vol. 22 **p.** 58
Pork country style	Vol. 4 **p.** 80
Pork (Crown roast of)	Vol. 4 **p.** 104
Pork (Glazed—roast)	Vol. 4 **p.** 24
Pork (Golden—chops)	Vol. 4 **p.** 50
Pork (Ground—with broccoli)	Vol. 18 **p.** 48
Pork (Homemade—rillettes)	Vol. 4 **p.** 82
Pork (Hot'n spicy—chops)	Vol. 4 **p.** 62
Pork kebabs	Vol. 4 **p.** 66
Pork Kiang	Vol. 18 **p.** 45
Pork (Lettuce leaves stuffed with)	Vol. 18 **p.** 42
Pork (Marinated—tenderloin with rice)	Vol. 18 **p.** 38
Pork meatballs	Vol. 18 **p.** 46
Pork (Medallions of—with Bordelaise sauce)	Vol. 4 **p.** 76
Pork (Medallions of—with fennel)	Vol. 4 **p.** 78
Pork (Neapolitan—chops)	Vol. 4 **p.** 64
Pork pâté	Vol. 22 **p.** 24
Pork pâté *with bacon and pork liver*	Vol. 4 **p.** 74
Pork (Rice with—and vegetables)	Vol. 12 **p.** 76
Pork (Roast)	Vol. 25 **p.** 46
Pork (Roast—stuffed with prunes)	Vol. 4 **p.** 30
Pork (Roast—with potatoes)	Vol. 4 **p.** 22
Pork (Sauerkraut and)	Vol. 4 **p.** 94
Pork (Sliced—tenderloin with fine herbs)	Vol. 4 **p.** 72
Pork (Spanish—roast)	Vol. 4 **p.** 28
Pork spread	Vol. 23 **p.** 60
Pork surprise	Vol. 4 **p.** 52
Pork (Sweet and sour—chops)	Vol. 4 **p.** 68
Pork tenderloin Chiang Yu Wong	Vol. 18 **p.** 50
Pork tenderloin Oriental style	Vol. 22 **p.** 62
Pork Tsung	Vol. 18 **p.** 26
Pork (Veal and—terrine with cognac)	Vol. 23 **p.** 74
Pork with fine herbs	Vol. 14 **p.** 42
Pork with leeks	Vol. 14 **p.** 40
Pork with red peppers	Vol. 14 **p.** 44
Pork with sweet potatoes	Vol. 4 **p.** 83
Pork with water chestnuts	Vol. 24 **p.** 66
Potato and parsnip gratin	Vol. 25 **p.** 101
Potato (Cream of leek and—soup)	Vol. 11 **p.** 72
Potato (Prawns in—boats)	Vol. 6 **p.** 46
Potato salad with shrimps	Vol. 23 **p.** 70
Potato (Salmon-stuffed—boats)	Vol. 23 **p.** 91
Potatoes (Baked)	Vol. 13 **p.** 32

Potatoes (Baked—in their jackets)	Vol. 20 **p.**	**28**
Potatoes (Parsley)	Vol. 13 **p.**	**28**
Potatoes (Pork and—with sweet sauce)	Vol. 24 **p.**	**78**
Potatoes (Pork with sweet)	Vol. 4 **p.**	**83**
Potatoes (Roast pork with)	Vol. 4 **p.**	**22**
Potatoes (Scalloped)	Vol. 13 **p.**	**36**
Potatoes (Stuffed)	Vol. 13 **p.**	**30**
Potatoes stuffed with sardines	Vol. 15 **p.**	**58**
Potatoes stuffed with sour cream and cheese	Vol. 15 **p.**	**102**
Potatoes with a garlic stuffing	Vol. 15 **p.**	**103**
Potatoes with onions	Vol. 13 **p.**	**40**
Potatoes with veal stock	Vol. 13 **p.**	**34**
Potatoes ("Two-step")	Vol. 13 **p.**	**38**
Prawn risotto	Vol. 24 **p.**	**28**
Prawns in potato boats	Vol. 6 **p.**	**46**
Prawns Italian style	Vol. 6 **p.**	**45**
Prawns with garlic butter	Vol. 6 **p.**	**42**
Provençale sauce	Vol. 11 **p.**	**25**
Prunes (Pork chops with)	Vol. 22 **p.**	**58**
Pudding (Black magic)	Vol. 9 **p.**	**69**
Pudding (Bread)	Vol. 9 **p.**	**70**
Pudding (Cheesy)	Vol. 20 **p.**	**52**
Pudding (Festive)	Vol. 23 **p.**	**96**
Pudding (Lazy)	Vol. 3 **p.**	**78**
Pudding (Lemon and pineapple)	Vol. 9 **p.**	**71**
Pudding (Plum)	Vol. 24 **p.**	**54**
Pudding (Rice)	Vol. 9 **p.**	**66**
Pudding (Rum—flambé)	Vol. 3 **p.**	**76**
Pudding (Snowball)	Vol. 3 **p.**	**79**
Pudding (Tapioca)	Vol. 9 **p.**	**68**
Pumpkin pie	Vol. 25 **p.**	**79**
Pumpkin soup	Vol. 19 **p.**	**26**
Punch (Champagne)	Vol. 23 **p.**	**104**
Punch (Christmas)	Vol. 25 **p.**	**17**
Punch (Festive fruit)	Vol. 23 **p.**	**76**
Punch (Flamboyant)	Vol. 25 **p.**	**15**
Punch (Fruit)	Vol. 23 **p.**	**86**
Punch (Fruit) *with white wine*	Vol. 25 **p.**	**16**
Punch (Golden)	Vol. 25 **p.**	**15**
Punch (Hot fruit)	Vol. 20 **p.**	**76**
Punch (Japanese)	Vol. 25 **p.**	**17**
Punch (Pineapple and strawberry)	Vol. 23 **p.**	**97**
Purée of pea soup	Vol. 11 **p.**	**67**

Q

Quail casserole with peas	Vol. 7	p. 61
Quails hunter style	Vol. 17	p. 54
Quails in wine	Vol. 23	p. 103
Quails with green grapes	Vol. 2	p. 46
Quails with onion	Vol. 7	p. 54
Quails with white wine	Vol. 7	p. 56
Queen Elizabeth cake	Vol. 3	p. 62
Quiche (Broccoli and cheese)	Vol. 16	p. 86
Quiche (Cabbage)	Vol. 13	p. 54
Quiche (Cauliflower)	Vol. 15	p. 72
Quiche (Chicken and broccoli)	Vol. 2	p. 86
Quiche (Crab)	Vol. 16	p. 88
Quiche (Hamburger)	Vol. 8	p. 90
Quiche (Rice)	Vol. 12	p. 74
Quiche (Seafood)	Vol. 6	p. 90
Quiche (Tofu)	Vol. 13	p. 101
Quiche (Vegetable)	Vol. 23	p. 62
Quick bread (Apple)	Vol. 9	p. 25
Quick bread dough	Vol. 9	p. 22
Quick bread ring with nuts and green cherries	Vol. 9	p. 23

R

Rabbit with coconut	Vol. 24 p.	80
Rabbit with mustard	Vol. 25 p.	56
Rabbit with white wine	Vol. 24 p.	20
Rack of lamb French style	Vol. 10 p.	88
Ragoût of lamb	Vol. 10 p.	96
Raisin (Apple and—cake)	Vol. 19 p.	90
Raisin (Old-fashioned—cookies)	Vol. 3 p.	26
Raisin sauce	Vol. 11 p.	54
Raisins (Peaches stuffed with almonds and)	Vol. 19 p.	92
Ramekins (Beef)	Vol. 1 p.	76
Ramekins (Veal)	Vol. 19 p.	53
Raspberries (Guinea fowl with)	Vol. 7 p.	104
Raspberry jam	Vol. 9 p.	96
Raspberry coulis (Poached pears with)	Vol. 5 p.	105
Ratatouille	Vol. 13 p.	66
Ratatouille with chick peas	Vol. 19 p.	42
Ravioli in soup	Vol. 12 p.	56
Ravioli with scallops and fennel	Vol. 12 p.	58
Red mullet en papillote	Vol. 5 p.	90
Red mullet with lemon and chives	Vol. 24 p.	50
Red sauce	Vol. 18 p.	72
Rhubarb compote	Vol. 9 p.	92
Rhubarb tart	Vol. 23 p.	46
Ribs (Short—Korean style)	Vol. 24 p.	68
Ribs with barbecue sauce	Vol. 1 p.	36
Rice and lobster salad	Vol. 12 p.	84
Rice and orange stuffing	Vol. 12 p.	80
Rice and vegetable casserole	Vol. 12 p.	88
Rice and vegetable stuffing	Vol. 12 p.	78
Rice (Chicken and—casserole)	Vol. 18 p.	80
Rice (Cheese and—loaf)	Vol. 16 p.	96
Rice (Chicken and—soup)	Vol. 11 p.	91
Rice (Chicken and—vol-au-vent)	Vol. 12 p.	96
Rice (Chicken, ham and—soup)	Vol. 24 p.	83
Rice (Chicken liver and—soup)	Vol. 11 p.	86
Rice (Chicken—pilaf)	Vol. 2 p.	59
Rice (Creamed—with peaches)	Vol. 19 p.	96
Rice (Fried—with ham and eggs)	Vol. 18 p.	78
Rice (Fried—with shrimp)	Vol. 12 p.	70
Rice (Fried—with soy sauce)	Vol. 18 p.	74
Rice (Indian)	Vol. 12 p.	86
Rice (Julienne of veal with)	Vol. 14 p.	82
Rice (Lemon)	Vol. 12 p.	82
Rice (Marinated pork tenderloin with)	Vol. 18 p.	38
Rice pilaf	Vol. 1 p.	101

Alphabetical Index

Rice pudding	Vol. 9 p. 66	
Rice quiche	Vol. 23 p. 90	
Rice (Saffron)	Vol. 12 p. 90	
Rice salad	Vol. 23 p. 100	
Rice (Scrambled eggs with)	Vol. 16 p. 53	
Rice (Steamed)	Vol. 18 p. 101	
Rice (Tomatoes stuffed with)	Vol. 15 p. 62	
Rice (Tsung fried)	Vol. 18 p. 76	
Rice (Vegetable and—salad)	Vol. 23 p. 101	
Rice (Wild)	Vol. 12 p. 72	
Rice with almonds	Vol. 12 p. 83	
Rice with chicken	Vol. 12 p. 94	
Rice with noodles	Vol. 20 p. 40	
Rice with pork and vegetables	Vol. 12 p. 76	
Rice with tofu, Oriental style	Vol. 19 p. 46	
Rice with vegetables	Vol. 22 p. 88	
Risotto Milanese style	Vol. 12 p. 92	
Risotto (Shrimp)	Vol. 19 p. 76	
Roast bear	Vol. 17 p. 92	
Roast beef	Vol. 25 p. 66	
Roast beef with herbs	Vol. 8 p. 22	
Roast beef with mustard sauce	Vol. 23 p. 72	
Roast (Blade)	Vol. 8 p. 40	
Roast (Boneless shoulder)	Vol. 8 p. 24	
Roast caribou	Vol. 17 p. 88	
Roast chicken with oregano	Vol. 7 p. 74	
Roast (Chuck)	Vol. 1 p. 38	
Roast (Cross rib)	Vol. 1 p. 32	
Roast duck in sauce piquante	Vol. 7 p. 48	
Roast duck stuffed with oysters	Vol. 17 p. 52	
Roast duck with orange sauce	Vol. 2 p. 44	
Roast lamb with Madeira	Vol. 10 p. 84	
Roast leg of deer	Vol. 17 p. 78	
Roast loin of veal	Vol. 10 p. 20	
Roast moose	Vol. 17 p. 68	
Roast pork	Vol. 25 p. 46	
Roast pork stuffed with prunes	Vol. 4 p. 30	
Roast pork with potatoes	Vol. 4 p. 22	
Roast (Rolled sirloin)	Vol. 1 p. 30	
Roast turkey	Vol. 2 p. 24	
Roast veal shoulder with cabbage	Vol. 10 p. 24	
Rolled roast of veal	Vol. 10 p. 22	
Rolled sirloin roast	Vol. 1 p. 30	
Rolled turkey roast with herbs	Vol. 2 p. 34	
Roquefort (Fettuccine with—cheese)	Vol. 12 p. 46	
Rosy dip	Vol. 16 p. 105	
Rosy sauce	Vol. 11 p. 38	
Rum babas	Vol. 9 p. 74	
Rum pudding flambé	Vol. 3 p. 76	
Rutabaga and green pepper with cheese	Vol. 13 p. 53	
Rutabaga (Cream of—soup)	Vol. 21 p. 30	

S

Saffron chicken	Vol. 2 p. 52
Saffron rice	Vol. 12 p. 90
Salad (Artichoke and mushroom)	Vol. 13 p. 86
Salad (Beef)	Vol. 14 p. 76
Salad (Brown rice and mushroom)	Vol. 12 p. 101
Salad (Chef's)	Vol. 4 p. 100
Salad (Chicken)	Vol. 2 p. 57
Salad (Christmas)	Vol. 25 p. 96
Salad (Country)	Vol. 23 p. 60
Salad (Crabmeat—on croissants)	Vol. 6 p. 64
Salad (Cucumber)	Vol. 23 p. 40
Salad (Cucumber) *with English cucumbers*	Vol. 10 p. 100
Salad (Fruit)	Vol. 8 p. 105
Salad (Fruit) *fruit and canteloupes*	Vol. 23 p. 67
Salad (Green)	Vol. 25 p. 42
Salad (Green—with herbs)	Vol. 23 p. 50
Salad (Hot fruit)	Vol. 23 p. 105
Salad (Lotus root)	Vol. 18 p. 96
Salad (Macaroni)	Vol. 23 p. 30
Salad (Mushroom and cauliflower)	Vol. 22 p. 101
Salad (Pineapple)	Vol. 23 p. 46
Salad (Pineapple fruit)	Vol. 9 p. 58
Salad (Potato—with shrimps)	Vol. 23 p. 70
Salad (Rice)	Vol. 23 p. 100
Salad (Rice and lobster)	Vol. 12 p. 84
Salad (Seafood)	Vol. 6 p. 48
Salad (Spinach)	Vol. 8 p. 101
Salad (Tomato)	Vol. 23 p. 60
Salad (Tomato—Italian style)	Vol. 23 p. 70
Salad (Vegetable and rice)	Vol. 23 p. 101
Salisbury steak	Vol. 8 p. 54
Salmon and cheese loaf	Vol. 14 p. 88
Salmon (Egg and—loaf)	Vol. 23 p. 34
Salmon (Lasagna with)	Vol. 12 p. 40
Salmon loaf	Vol. 20 p. 68
Salmon manicotti	Vol. 5 p. 34
Salmon mousse	Vol. 22 p. 26
Salmon omelette	Vol. 16 p. 36
Salmon pie	Vol. 5 p. 30
Salmon ring loaf	Vol. 5 p. 36
Salmon (Scrambled eggs with smoked)	Vol. 16 p. 50
Salmon steaks with duxelles	Vol. 5 p. 32
Salmon-stuffed potato boats	Vol. 23 p. 91
Salmon trout with red wine	Vol. 5 p. 104
Salmon vol-au-vent	Vol. 8 p. 100
Salmon (Whole—stuffed with shrimp)	Vol. 5 p. 28
Salmon with armagnac	Vol. 25 p. 34
Salmon with dill sauce	Vol. 21 p. 80
Sandwich (Hot chicken)	Vol. 7 p. 86
Sandwich (Hot ham)	Vol. 14 p. 100
Sandwich (Mexican-style pita)	Vol. 19 p. 72
Sandwich (Turkey)	Vol. 7 p. 30
Sandwiches (Pita—with lamb meatballs)	Vol. 21 p. 70
Sangria	Vol. 25 p. 17
Sardine appetizer	Vol. 15 p. 30
Sardines (Potatoes stuffed with)	Vol. 15 p. 58
Sauce (Anchovy)	Vol. 11 p. 42
Sauce (Asparagus with Mornay or Béarnaise)	Vol. 15 p. 54
Sauce (Barbecue)	Vol. 11 p. 48
Sauce Bâtarde	Vol. 11 p. 36
Sauce (Béarnaise)	Vol. 1 p. 35
Sauce (Béchamel)	Vol. 11 p. 13
Sauce (Béchamel—with peppers)	Vol. 11 p. 28
Sauce (Bordelaise)	Vol. 1 p. 34
Sauce (Bread)	Vol. 11 p. 28
Sauce (Brown)	Vol. 11 p. 48
Sauce (Butter and dill)	Vol. 11 p. 18
Sauce (Caper)	Vol. 11 p. 25
Sauce (Chicken velouté)	Vol. 11 p. 28
Sauce (Clam)	Vol. 11 p. 44
Sauce (Cranberry)	Vol. 11 p. 30
Sauce (Cranberry and pear)	Vol. 2 p. 101
Sauce (Cucumber and dill)	Vol. 11 p. 18
Sauce (Curry)	Vol. 11 p. 30
Sauce (Deviled)	Vol. 11 p. 32
Sauce (Eggs poached in tomato)	Vol. 16 p. 45
Sauce (Espagnole)	Vol. 11 p. 22
Sauce (Fennel)	Vol. 11 p. 48
Sauce (Fish stock)	Vol. 16 p. 58
Sauce (Hollandaise)	Vol. 11 p. 12
Sauce (Hollandaise Chantilly)	Vol. 11 p. 36
Sauce (Horseradish)	Vol. 11 p. 24

Sauce (Italian)	Vol. 1 p. **88**
Sauce (Italian vegetable)	Vol. 16 p. **59**
Sauce (Italian) *with meatballs*	Vol. 11 p. **50**
Sauce (Lemon)	Vol. 11 p. **20**
Sauce (Lemon butter)	Vol. 11 p. **36**
Sauce (Lichee)	Vol. 18 p. **70**
Sauce (Madeira)	Vol. 11 p. **32**
Sauce (Mariana)	Vol. 11 p. **43**
Sauce (Mornay)	Vol. 11 p. **14**
Sauce (Mustard)	Vol. 11 p. **22**
Sauce (Newburg)	Vol. 11 p. **24**
Sauce (Parmesan)	Vol. 11 p. **22**
Sauce (Parmesan white)	Vol. 16 p. **58**
Sauce (Peppercorn)	Vol. 11 p. **48**
Sauce (Plum)	Vol. 18 p. **68**
Sauce (Polonaise)	Vol. 11 p. **38**
Sauce (Provençale)	Vol. 11 p. **25**
Sauce (Raisin)	Vol. 11 p. **54**
Sauce (Red)	Vol. 18 p. **72**
Sauce (Rosy)	Vol. 11 p. **38**

Sauce (Soubise)	Vol. 11 p. **24**
Sauce (Sour cream)	Vol. 11 p. **36**
Sauce (Spinach)	Vol. 11 p. **43**
Sauce (Sweet and sour)	Vol. 11 p. **18**
Sauce (Sweet and sour) *with pineapple*	Vol. 1 p. **89**
Sauce (Tartar)	Vol. 11 p. **18**
Sauce (Teriyaki)	Vol. 11 p. **50**
Sauce (Tomato)	Vol. 11 p. **42**
Sauce (Vaucluse)	Vol. 11 p. **28**
Sauce (Velouté)	Vol. 16 p. **58**
Sauces for duck	Vol. 17 p. **58**
Sauerkraut and pork	Vol. 4 p. **94**
Sauerkraut (Partridge with)	Vol. 17 p. **32**
Sausage (Cornish game hens with—stuffing)	Vol. 7 p. **64**
Sausage fricassee	Vol. 4 p. **90**
Sausage kebabs	Vol. 20 p. **56**
Sausage meatballs	Vol. 14 p. **80**
Sausages and bacon	Vol. 23 p. **80**

Alphabetical Index

Sausages (Beef)	Vol. 8 p. 74
Sausages with apple slices	Vol. 4 p. 88
Scalloped potatoes	Vol. 13 p. 36
Scallops in tomato sauce	Vol. 15 p. 24
Scallops on the half shell	Vol. 6 p. 53
Scallops (Ravioli with—and fennel)	Vol. 12 p. 58
Scallops Tsao Ku	Vol. 18 p. 61
Scallops with almonds	Vol. 14 p. 92
Scallops with lemon and spinach	Vol. 19 p. 78
Scallops with vegetables	Vol. 21 p. 78
Scones	Vol. 21 p. 94
Scrambled egg tartlets	Vol. 16 p. 64
Scrambled eggs with rice	Vol. 16 p. 53
Scrambled eggs with smoked salmon	Vol. 16 p. 50
Sea pike in caper sauce	Vol. 5 p. 96
Seafood (Avocados with)	Vol. 15 p. 98
Seafood casserole	Vol. 6 p. 88
Seafood chowder	Vol. 11 p. 76
Seafood en coquille	Vol. 16 p. 80
Seafood (Fettuccine with)	Vol. 6 p. 83
Seafood hors d'oeuvres	Vol. 6 p. 92
Seafood kebabs	Vol. 6 p. 76
Seafood quiche	Vol. 6 p. 90
Seafood salad	Vol. 6 p. 48
Seafood (Spaghettini with)	Vol. 6 p. 82
Seafood stew	Vol. 24 p. 100
Seafood vol-au-vent	Vol. 6 p. 80
Shank of lamb European style	Vol. 10 p. 80
Shepherd's pie	Vol. 1 p. 93
Shortcake (Strawberry)	Vol. 3 p. 60
Shrimp au gratin	Vol. 15 p. 22
Shrimp bisque	Vol. 11 p. 80
Shrimp (Couscous with chicken and—)	Vol. 2 p. 96
Shrimp Creole	Vol. 21 p. 74
Shrimp (Fried rice with)	Vol. 12 p. 70
Shrimp in baskets	Vol. 25 p. 84
Shrimp Kiang	Vol. 18 p. 58
Shrimp pâté	Vol. 25 p. 102
Shrimp (Peach halves with—mousse)	Vol. 22 p. 100
Shrimp (Pizza with)	Vol. 14 p. 105
Shrimp risotto	Vol. 19 p. 76
Shrimp (Sole fillets stuffed with)	Vol. 22 p. 72
Shrimp (Vegetable and—platter)	Vol. 23 p. 21
Shrimp with feta cheese in tomato sauce	Vol. 19 p. 82
Shrimps American style	Vol. 6 p. 38
Shrimps Chinese style	Vol. 6 p. 36
Shrimps (Linguine with—and tomatoes)	Vol. 21 p. 82
Shrimps (Potato salad with)	Vol. 23 p. 70
Shrimps with coconut	Vol. 6 p. 40
Shrimps with garlic butter	Vol. 6 p. 34
Short ribs Korean style	Vol. 24 p. 68
Sirloin steak London style	Vol. 8 p. 45
Sliced pork tenderloin with fine herbs	Vol. 4 p. 72
Smelts in a rosy sauce	Vol. 5 p. 82
Smoked haddock	Vol. 24 p. 56
Snack (Hot)	Vol. 16 p. 100
Snow peas (Chicken soup with)	Vol. 18 p. 83
Snowball pudding	Vol. 3 p. 79
Sole (Fillet of—Creole style)	Vol. 22 p. 74
Sole (Fillets of—breaded Italian style)	Vol. 5 p. 46
Sole (Fillets of—with almonds)	Vol. 5 p. 45
Sole fillets stuffed with shrimp	Vol. 22 p. 72
Sole mousse	Vol. 25 p. 94
Sole roulades with a tropical sauce	Vol. 5 p. 48
Sole (Stuffed fillets of)	Vol. 5 p. 42
Sorbet (Mandarin and ginger)	Vol. 9 p. 62
Sorbet (Strawberry)	Vol. 2 p. 105
Sorbet (Tomato)	Vol. 6 p. 100
Soubise sauce	Vol. 11 p. 24
Soufflé (Tomato)	Vol. 22 p. 30
Soufflé (Pizza)	Vol. 16 p. 90
Sauce (Asparagus with mustard)	Vol. 4 p. 101
Soup (Beef)	Vol. 21 p. 26
Soup (Broad bean)	Vol. 19 p. 24
Soup (Broccoli and onion)	Vol. 19 p. 30
Soup (Cabbage)	Vol. 11 p. 93
Soup (Carrot)	Vol. 21 p. 32
Soup (Celery)	Vol. 19 p. 34
Soup (Cheese)	Vol. 16 p. 76
Soup (Chicken and ham)	Vol. 11 p. 84
Soup (Chicken and rice)	Vol. 11 p. 91
Soup (Chicken liver and rice)	Vol. 11 p. 86
Soup (Chicken noodle)	Vol. 11 p. 90
Soup (Chicken—with snow peas)	Vol. 18 p. 83
Soup (Cod)	Vol. 11 p. 78
Soup (Cold)	Vol. 11 p. 100
Soup (Corn)	Vol. 18 p. 82
Soup (Crab)	Vol. 21 p. 28
Soup (Cream of asparagus)	Vol. 5 p. 100
Soup (Cream of carrot) *beef bouillon*	Vol. 25 p. 74
Soup (Cream of carrot) *chicken stock*	Vol. 12 p. 100
Soup (Cream of cauliflower)	Vol. 11 p. 66
Soup (Cream of celery)	Vol. 6 p. 101
Soup (Cream of cucumber and artichoke)	Vol. 11 p. 72
Soup (Cream of leek and broccoli)	Vol. 21 p. 36
Soup (Cream of leek and potato)	Vol. 11 p. 72
Soup (Cream of lobster)	Vol. 11 p. 76
Soup (Cream of mushroom)	Vol. 11 p. 68
Soup (Cream of rutabaga)	Vol. 21 p. 30
Soup (Cucumber and tomato)	Vol. 21 p. 24
Soup (Chicken, ham and rice)	Vol. 24 p. 83
Soup (Curried apple)	Vol. 25 p. 32
Soup (Egg and lemon)	Vol. 24 p. 36
Soup (Fish and leek)	Vol. 11 p. 78
Soup (Fisherman's)	Vol. 19 p. 28
Soup (Gazpacho)	Vol. 11 p. 102
Soup (Ham and watercress)	Vol. 11 p. 84
Soup (Home-style soup)	Vol. 11 p. 98
Soup (Leek)	Vol. 1 p. 100
Soup (Lentil)	Vol. 11 p. 92
Soup (Lentil) *with red lentils and potatoes*	Vol. 13 p. 100
Soup (Lentil and tomato)	Vol. 19 p. 32
Soup (Minestrone) *beef stock*	Vol. 11 p. 96
Soup (Minestrone) *chicken bouillon*	Vol. 21 p. 34
Soup (Onion—au gratin)	Vol. 11 p. 94
Soup (Oyster)	Vol. 11 p. 80
Soup (Pea)	Vol. 11 p. 96
Soup (Pear and watercress)	Vol. 11 p. 102
Soup (Pumpkin)	Vol. 19 p. 26
Soup (Purée of pea)	Vol. 11 p. 67
Soup (Ravioli in)	Vol. 12 p. 56

Soup (Tomato and noodle)	Vol. 11 p. 88
Soup (Vegetable)	Vol. 11 p. 88
Soup (Vegetable) *with leeks and peppers*	Vol. 2 p. 100
Soup (Watercress)	Vol. 23 p. 30
Soup (Watercress) *with cream*	Vol. 20 p. 20
Soup (Winter melon)	Vol. 18 p. 96
Sour cream (Brussels sprouts with)	Vol. 13 p. 60
Sour cream (Chicken with)	Vol. 7 p. 96
Sour cream (Potatoes stuffed with—and cheese)	Vol. 15 p. 102
Sour cream sauce	Vol. 11 p. 36
Sour cream (Trout with)	Vol. 5 p. 40
Soy sauce (Fried rice with)	Vol. 18 p. 74
Spaghetti carbonara	Vol. 12 p. 24
Spaghetti with clam sauce	Vol. 12 p. 26
Spaghetti with meatballs and tomato sauce	Vol. 12 p. 22
Spaghetti with tuna sauce	Vol. 12 p. 28
Spaghettini with eggplant	Vol. 14 p. 96
Spaghettini with garlic	Vol. 12 p. 30
Spaghettini with seafood	Vol. 6 p. 82
Spaghettini with vegetables	Vol. 20 p. 72
Spanish omelette	Vol. 16 p. 34
Spanish pork roast	Vol. 4 p. 28
Spareribs Chinese style	Vol. 18 p. 40
Spareribs with sweet and sour sauce	Vol. 22 p. 56
Spicy beef soup	Vol. 24 p. 72
Spicy frankfurters	Vol. 15 p. 45
Spinach and veal filling	Vol. 12 p. 52
Spinach (Cannelloni with veal and)	Vol. 12 p. 50
Spinach garnish	Vol. 16 p. 60
Spinach lasagna Bolognese	Vol. 12 p. 36
Spinach (Norway haddock fillets on a bed of)	Vol. 5 p. 64
Spinach (Manicotti with)	Vol. 19 p. 84
Spinach (Meat loaf with)	Vol. 1 p. 80
Spinach purée	Vol. 13 p. 72
Spinach salad	Vol. 8 p. 101
Spinach sauce	Vol. 11 p. 43
Spinach (Scallops with lemon and)	Vol. 19 p. 78
Spinach (Turkey roulades with—filling)	Vol. 2 p. 38
Spinach (Veal breast stuffed with—and ham)	Vol. 10 p. 104
Springtime omelette	Vol. 16 p. 30
Squares (Date)	Vol. 3 p. 105
Squares (Marshmallow)	Vol. 20 p. 86
Squid stuffed with ham	Vol. 6 p. 86
Steak hunter's style	Vol. 8 p. 69
Steak (Marinated)	Vol. 8 p. 72
Steak (Pepper)	Vol. 8 p. 32
Steak (Salisbury)	Vol. 8 p. 54
Steak (Sirloin—London style)	Vol. 8 p. 45
Steak Southern style	Vol. 14 p. 74
Steak Sukiyaki	Vol. 1 p. 42
Steak (T-bone)	Vol. 1 p. 64
Steak with Madeira sauce	Vol. 8 p. 36
Steak with tangy sauce	Vol. 8 p. 34
Steamed clams Oriental style	Vol. 6 p. 68
Steamed clams with garlic butter	Vol. 6 p. 66
Steamed rice	Vol. 18 p. 101

Stew (Bear)	Vol. 17 p. **94**	Stuffed artichokes	Vol. 13 p. **84**
Stew (Codfish)	Vol. 14 p. **90**	Stuffed beef heart	Vol. 8 p. **105**
Stew (Deer meat)	Vol. 17 p. **86**	Stuffed bread	Vol. 25 p. **20**
Stew (Fisherman's)	Vol. 19 p. **80**	Stuffed cabbage rolls	Vol. 1 p. **70**
Stew (Goose)	Vol. 17 p. **62**	Stuffed cornish game hen	Vol. 22 p. **50**
Stew (Ground beef)	Vol. 8 p. **56**	Stuffed fillets of sole	Vol. 5 p. **42**
Stew (Hunter's)	Vol. 24 p. **46**	Stuffed lobster tails	Vol. 6 p. **30**
Stew (Lamb)	Vol. 10 p. **83**	Stuffed mushroom caps	Vol. 23 p. **100**
Stew (Mexican beef)	Vol. 19 p. **66**	Stuffed mushroom caps *with celery*	Vol. 21 p. **50**
Stew (Moose)	Vol. 17 p. **70**	Stuffed onions	Vol. 13 p. **92**
Stew (New England)	Vol. 24 p. **94**	Stuffed pepper canapés	Vol. 13 p. **80**
Stew (Pigs' trotters)	Vol. 25 p. **98**	Stuffed peppers	Vol. 1 p. **95**
Stew (Pigs' trotters) *Quebec*	Vol. 24 p. **102**	Stuffed potatoes	Vol. 13 p. **30**
Stew (Seafood)	Vol. 24 p. **100**	Stuffed roast chicken	Vol. 7 p. **45**
Stew (Turkey)	Vol. 2 p. **32**	Stuffed tomatoes	Vol. 17 p. **104**
Stew (Vegetable)	Vol. 1 p. **62**	Stuffed turkey	Vol. 2 p. **104**
Stock (Chicken)	Vol. 11 p. **58**	Stuffed vine leaves	Vol. 15 p. **42**
Stock (Fish)	Vol. 11 p. **59**	Stuffed zucchini	Vol. 13 p. **68**
Stock (Meat)	Vol. 11 p. **58**	Stuffing (Rice and orange)	Vol. 12 p. **80**
Stock (Vegetable)	Vol. 11 p. **59**	Stuffing (Rice and vegetable)	Vol. 12 p. **78**
Strawberry cream	Vol. 3 p. **82**	Stuffing (Turkey with cornbread)	Vol. 7 p. **22**
Strawberry jam	Vol. 9 p. **94**	Stuffings for game	Vol. 17 p. **57**
Strawberry-lime chiffon cake	Vol. 23 p. **36**	Sugar pie	Vol. 3 p. **88**
Strawberry mousse	Vol. 3 p. **102**	Summer vegetable combination	Vol. 13 p. **96**
Strawberry pie	Vol. 3 p. **90**	Sweet and sour pork chops	Vol. 4 p. **68**
Strawberry (Pineapple and—punch)	Vol. 23 p. **97**	Sweet and sour sauce	Vol. 11 p. **18**
Strawberry shortcake	Vol. 3 p. **60**	Sweet and sour sauce *with pineapple*	Vol. 1 p. **89**
Strawberry shortcake *individual*		Sweet dough	Vol. 9 p. **28**
servings	Vol. 22 p. **92**	Swiss fondue	Vol. 16 p. **66**
Strawberry sorbet	Vol. 2 p. **105**		
Strawberry trifle	Vol. 23 p. **47**		

T

Tagliatelle with tomato sauce	Vol. 24 p. 30
Tapioca pudding	Vol. 9 p. 68
Tart (Fruit)	Vol. 21 p. 92
Tart (Fruit and pecan)	Vol. 13 p. 105
Tart (Rhubarb)	Vol. 23 p. 46
Tartar sauce	Vol. 11 p. 18
Tarts (Coconut)	Vol. 18 p. 92
T-bone steak	Vol. 1 p. 64
Teriyaki sauce	Vol. 11 p. 50
Terrine (Broccoli)	Vol. 21 p. 42
Terrine (Veal and pork—with cognac)	Vol. 23 p. 74
Three-vegetable garnish	Vol. 13 p. 42
Tofu cheesecake	Vol. 21 p. 100
Tofu quiche	Vol. 13 p. 101
Tofu (Rice with—Oriental style)	Vol. 19 p. 46
Tomato and noodle soup	Vol. 11 p. 88
Tomato cake	Vol. 9 p. 44
Tomato (Cheese and—flan)	Vol. 16 p. 92
Tomato cocktail	Vol. 23 p. 66
Tomato (Cucumber and—soup)	Vol. 21 p. 24
Tomato (Eggplant and—fricassee)	Vol. 15 p. 64
Tomato (Green beans with—sauce)	Vol. 13 p. 62
Tomato ketchup	Vol. 13 p. 74
Tomato (Lentil and—soup)	Vol. 19 p. 32
Tomato mousse	Vol. 13 p. 82
Tomato (Onion and—casserole)	Vol. 13 p. 78
Tomato salad	Vol. 23 p. 60
Tomato salad Italian style	Vol. 23 p. 70
Tomato sauce	Vol. 11 p. 42
Tomato sorbet	Vol. 6 p. 100
Tomato soufflé	Vol. 22 p. 30
Tomatoes (Linguine with shrimps and)	Vol. 21 p. 82
Tomatoes (Onions with—and cream)	Vol. 15 p. 80
Tomatoes (Perch with)	Vol. 5 p. 72
Tomatoes Provençale	Vol. 13 p. 76
Tomatoes (Stuffed)	Vol. 17 p. 104
Tomatoes stuffed with eggs	Vol. 16 p. 61
Tomatoes stuffed with rice	Vol. 15 p. 62
Tomatoes stuffed with turkey	Vol. 2 p. 41
Tomatoes (Zucchini and—in scallop shells)	Vol. 19 p. 50
Topping (Chocolate)	Vol. 3 p. 72
Topping (Lemon)	Vol. 3 p. 73
Topping (Vanilla)	Vol. 3 p. 72
Tortellini with cream	Vol. 12 p. 54
Tourtière	Vol. 25 p. 100
Tourtière (French-Canadian)	Vol. 4 p. 86
Trifle (Strawberry)	Vol. 23 p. 47
Trout au bleu	Vol. 5 p. 38
Trout Mi-Chiu	Vol. 18 p. 64
Trout with almonds	Vol. 24 p. 22
Trout with capers	Vol. 22 p. 104
Trout with sour cream	Vol. 5 p. 40
Truffles (Partridge with)	Vol. 17 p. 30
Tsung fried rice	Vol. 18 p. 76
Tuna and noodles	Vol. 14 p. 94
Tuna au gratin	Vol. 5 p. 80
Tuna (Braised)	Vol. 24 p. 84
Tuna Florentine	Vol. 19 p. 74
Tuna omelette	Vol. 5 p. 74
Tuna (Spaghetti with—sauce)	Vol. 12 p. 28
Tuna steaks with Hollandaise sauce	Vol. 5 p. 76
Tuna tetrazzini	Vol. 5 p. 78
Turkey (All-purpose—base)	Vol. 14 p. 28
Turkey and bacon croquettes	Vol. 2 p. 36
Turkey and cheese casserole	Vol. 14 p. 52
Turkey (Braised—with vegetables)	Vol. 2 p. 26
Turkey escallops	Vol. 2 p. 28
Turkey (Holiday)	Vol. 25 p. 24
Turkey (Marinated—cutlets)	Vol. 7 p. 28
Turkey (Oriental)	Vol. 2 p. 73
Turkey ring	Vol. 14 p. 46
Turkey (Roast)	Vol. 2 p. 24
Turkey (Rolled—roast with herbs)	Vol. 2 p. 34
Turkey roulades with spinach filling	Vol. 2 p. 38
Turkey sandwich	Vol. 7 p. 30
Turkey stew	Vol. 2 p. 32
Turkey (Stuffed)	Vol. 2 p. 104
Turkey-stuffed avocado	Vol. 14 p. 50
Turkey (Tomatoes stuffed with)	Vol. 2 p. 41
Turkey Véronique	Vol. 14 p. 48
Turkey with cornbread stuffing	Vol. 7 p. 22
Turkey with paprika	Vol. 2 p. 43
Turkey with vegetables	Vol. 7 p. 24
"Two-step" potatoes	Vol. 13 p. 38

V

Vanilla cream	Vol. 3 p. 81	
Vanilla topping	Vol. 3 p. 72	
Vaucluse sauce	Vol. 11 p. 28	
Veal and pork terrine with cognac	Vol. 23 p. 74	
Veal and vegetable loaf	Vol. 21 p. 66	
Veal (Blanquette of)	Vol. 10 p. 52	
Veal (Cannelloni with—and spinach)	Vol. 12 p. 50	
Veal casserole	Vol. 10 p. 28	
Veal Cordon Bleu	Vol. 10 p. 45	
Veal (Emincé of—with cream sauce)	Vol. 25 p. 76	
Veal escallops with mushrooms and wine	Vol. 19 p. 64	

Veal fricassee	Vol. 10 p. 54
Veal galantine	Vol. 10 p. 50
Veal (Julienne of—with rice)	Vol. 14 p. 82
Veal loaf	Vol. 10 p. 56
Veal Parmesan	Vol. 10 p. 42
Veal (Paupiettes of)	Vol. 10 p. 40
Veal (Potatoes with—stock)	Vol. 13 p. 34
Veal ramekins	Vol. 19 p. 53
Veal (Roast loin of)	Vol. 10 p. 20
Veal (Roast—shoulder with cabbage)	Vol. 10 p. 24
Veal (Rolled roast of)	Vol. 10 p. 22
Veal rolls	Vol. 24 p. 90

W-Z

Veal breast stuffed with spinach and ham	Vol. 10 **p. 104**
Veal rump roast with apples	Vol. 10 **p. 30**
Veal sauté Marengo	Vol. 10 **p. 48**
Veal scallopini with cream	Vol. 12 **p. 104**
Veal shank (Braised)	Vol. 10 **p. 36**
Veal (Spinach and—filling)	Vol. 12 **p. 52**
Veal with stewed fruit	Vol. 10 **p. 38**
Veal with vegetables	Vol. 22 **p. 80**
Vegetable and noodle soup	Vol. 20 **p. 24**
Vegetable and rice salad	Vol. 23 **p. 101**
Vegetable and shrimp platter	Vol. 23 **p. 21**
Vegetable paella	Vol. 21 **p. 61**
Vegetable quiche	Vol. 23 **p. 62**
Vegetable soup	Vol. 11 **p. 88**
Vegetable stew	Vol. 1 **p. 62**
Vegetable stock	Vol. 11 **p. 59**
Vegetable (Summer—combination)	Vol. 13 **p. 96**
Vegetable (Three-—garnish)	Vol. 13 **p. 42**
Vegetables au gratin	Vol. 16 **p. 94**
Vegetables (Braised)	Vol. 19 **p. 40**
Vegetables (Festive summer)	Vol. 15 **p. 66**
Vegetables (Fried—Chinese style)	Vol. 13 **p. 88**
Vegetables (Garden—with vinaigrette dressing)	Vol. 7 **p. 101**
Vegetables (Glazed)	Vol. 25 **p. 103**
Vegetables julienne	Vol. 23 **p. 80**
Vegetables (Macédoine of—with cheese)	Vol. 16 **p. 74**
Vegetables (Marinated)	Vol. 25 **p. 59**
Vegetables (Mixed)	Vol. 13 **p. 50**
Vegetables Oriental style	Vol. 15 **p. 90**
Velouté sauce	Vol. 16 **p. 58**
Vichy carrots	Vol. 25 **p. 27**
Vichyssoise	Vol. 19 **p. 36**
Vinaigrette (Garden vegetables with—dressing)	Vol. 7 **p. 101**
Vine leaves (Stuffed)	Vol. 15 **p. 42**
Vol-au-vent (Crab)	Vol. 15 **p. 32**
Vol-au-vent (Ham)	Vol. 4 **p. 48**
Vol-au-vent (Seafood)	Vol. 6 **p. 80**
Vol-au-vent (Salmon)	Vol. 8 **p. 100**
Vol-au-vents (Chicken and rice)	Vol. 12 **p. 96**
Water chestnuts (Pork with)	Vol. 24 **p. 66**
Watercress (Ham and—soup)	Vol. 11 **p. 84**
Watercress (Pear and—soup)	Vol. 11 **p. 102**
Watercress soup	Vol. 23 **p. 30**
Watercress soup *with cream*	Vol. 20 **p. 20**
Wheat germ muffins	Vol. 21 **p. 88**
White cake	Vol. 3 **p. 55**
Whole salmon stuffed with shrimp	Vol. 5 **p. 28**
Whole wheat banana bread	Vol. 3 **p. 34**
Whole wheat bread	Vol. 3 **p. 32**
Whole wheat honey muffins	Vol. 3 **p. 43**
Wiener schnitzel	Vol. 10 **p. 46**
Wild rice	Vol. 12 **p. 72**
Wine (Chicken with—and herbs)	Vol. 2 **p. 62**
Wine (Fettuccine with red)	Vol. 12 **p. 45**
Wine (Mulled)	Vol. 25 **p. 16**
Wine (Oranges in)	Vol. 21 **p. 96**
Wine (Partridge with red)	Vol. 17 **p. 28**
Wine (Pears in red)	Vol. 9 **p. 52**
Wine (Quails in)	Vol. 23 **p. 103**
Wine (Quails with white)	Vol. 7 **p. 56**
Wine (Salmon trout with red)	Vol. 5 **p. 104**
Wine (Veal escallops with mushrooms and)	Vol. 19 **p. 64**
Winter melon soup	Vol. 18 **p. 96**
Yellow beans Creole style	Vol. 13 **p. 61**
Yellow perch with beer	Vol. 5 **p. 84**
Yoghurt (Beef surprise with)	Vol. 8 **p. 53**
Yoghurt (Blueberries with—and honey)	Vol. 23 **p. 37**
Yoghurt (Chicken with)	Vol. 21 **p. 58**
Zucchini and tomatoes in scallop shells	Vol. 19 **p. 50**
Zucchini Greek style	Vol. 24 **p. 34**
Zucchini Italian style	Vol. 13 **p. 70**
Zucchini omelette	Vol. 16 **p. 28**
Zucchini Provençale	Vol. 21 **p. 53**
Zucchini (Stuffed)	Vol. 13 **p. 68**
Zucchini stuffed with veal	Vol. 15 **p. 38**
Zucchini with garlic	Vol. 25 **p. 89**

Thematic
Index

Anchovy	Anchovy sauce	Vol. 11 p.	42
Appetizers	Cheese ball	Vol. 16 p.	68
	Cold sauces for cold appetizers	Vol. 15 p.	14
	Coquilles Saint-Jacques	Vol. 15 p.	28
	Pork pâté	Vol. 14 p.	78
	Preparing hot appetizers	Vol. 15 p.	12
	Shrimp pâté	Vol. 25 p.	102
	Spicy frankfurters	Vol. 15 p.	45
	Stuffed mushroom caps	Vol. 23 p.	100
	Stuffed mushroom caps (with celery)	Vol. 21 p.	50
Beef	All-purpose ground beef base	Vol. 14 p.	24
	Appearance of beef	Vol. 1 p.	13
	Beef à la mode	Vol. 8 p.	30
	Beef and macaroni casserole with corn	Vol. 14 p.	32
	Beef and peppers	Vol. 18 p.	100
	Beef Bourguignon (double recipe)	Vol. 1 p.	56
	Beef Bourguignon (single recipe)	Vol. 22 p.	38
	Beef flank	Vol. 8 p.	42
	Beef goulash	Vol. 8 p.	83
	Beef in beer	Vol. 1 p.	58
	Beef in patty shells	Vol. 8 p.	92
	Beef kebabs	Vol. 1 p.	60
	Beef kidneys	Vol. 8 p.	80
	Beef liver in brown gravy	Vol. 1 p.	96
	Beef Niçoise	Vol. 8 p.	94
	Beef omelette	Vol. 1 p.	74
	Beef ramekins	Vol. 1 p.	76
	Beef roulades	Vol. 24 p.	40
	Beef roulades with mustard	Vol. 1 p.	48
	Beef salad	Vol. 14 p.	76
	Beef sausages	Vol. 8 p.	74
	Beef sauté with orange segments	Vol. 19 p.	68
	Beef soup	Vol. 21 p.	26
	Beef Stroganoff	Vol. 1 p.	40
	Beef surprise with yoghurt	Vol. 8 p.	53
	Beef tenderloin marinated in soy sauce	Vol. 1 p.	102
	Beef tongue with almonds	Vol. 8 p.	76
	Beef Wellington	Vol. 8 p.	46
	Beef with celery and bacon	Vol. 1 p.	54
	Beef with olives	Vol. 1 p.	68
	Beef with orange	Vol. 22 p.	34
	Beef with red peppers	Vol. 8 p.	48
	Beef with sliced peppers	Vol. 8 p.	78
	Blade roast	Vol. 8 p.	40
	Bologna and beef rolls	Vol. 22 p.	36
	Boneless shoulder roast	Vol. 8 p.	24
	Braised beef	Vol. 1 p.	66
	Buying and storing beef	Vol. 1 p.	15
	Cabbage rolls	Vol. 24 p.	48
	Characteristics of beef and microwaving	Vol. 1 p.	11
	Chart for cooking beef	Vol. 8 p.	13
	Cheesy beef pie	Vol. 8 p.	64

Beef   Chili   Vol. 1 p. 94

	Vol.	p.
Chili	Vol. 1	94
Chinese beef (with sake)	Vol. 1	52
Chinese beef (with soy sauce)	Vol. 21	62
Chinese beef casserole	Vol. 14	34
Chuck roast	Vol. 1	38
Cooking times	Vol. 1	22
Cross rib roast	Vol. 1	32
Curried beef	Vol. 14	30
Cuts of beef	Vol. 1	8
Defrosting	Vol. 1	19
Defrosting and cooking combined	Vol. 1	22
Deglazing	Vol. 1	35
Fillet mignon	Vol. 1	51
Frankfurters and beans	Vol. 8	96
Freezing beef	Vol. 8	18
Freezing ground beef	Vol. 1	73
Freezing irregularly shaped cuts	Vol. 1	15
Freezing meat loaf	Vol. 1	85
Grandmother's macaroni	Vol. 8	86
Ground beef base	Vol. 1	90
Ground beef casserole (with green beans)	Vol. 1	72
Ground beef casserole (with potatoes and carrots)	Vol. 22	40
Ground beef stew	Vol. 8	56
Hamburger quiche	Vol. 8	90
Hamburgers	Vol. 1	78
Interlarding	Vol. 8	27
Italian meat loaf	Vol. 8	82
Lasagna	Vol. 8	88
Macaroni stir-fry	Vol. 1	92
Macédoine of beef	Vol. 1	45
Marinated steak	Vol. 8	72
Meat loaf with barbecue flavor	Vol. 8	68
Meat loaf with chili sauce	Vol. 1	84
Meat loaf with pistachios	Vol. 24	62
Meat loaf with spinach	Vol. 1	80
Meat loaf with sweet and sour sauce	Vol. 1	83
Meat loaves	Vol. 1	82
Meatball kebabs	Vol. 1	86
Meatballs	Vol. 8	58
Meatballs with baked beans	Vol. 8	61
Mexican beef	Vol. 8	84
Mexican beef stew	Vol. 19	66
Moussaka	Vol. 8	62
New England braised beef	Vol. 8	28
New England stew (Corned beef)	Vol. 24	94
Old-fashioned meat loaf	Vol. 8	66
Oriental beef with mandarins	Vol. 8	50
Pepper steak	Vol. 8	32
Poached meatballs with lemon sauce	Vol. 24	42
Ribs with barbecue sauce	Vol. 1	36
Roast beef	Vol. 25	66

Beef	Roast beef with herbs	Vol. 8 p. 22
	Roast beef with mustard sauce	Vol. 23 p. 72
	Rolled sirloin roast	Vol. 1 p. 30
	Salisbury steak	Vol. 8 p. 54
	Shepherd's pie	Vol. 1 p. 93
	Short ribs Korean style	Vol. 24 p. 68
	Sirloin steak London style	Vol. 8 p. 45
	Spaghetti with meatballs and tomato sauce	Vol. 12 p. 22
	Spices, aromatics and condiments for beef	Vol. 1 p. 28
	Spicy beef soup	Vol. 24 p. 72
	Steak hunter's style	Vol. 8 p. 69
	Steak Southern style	Vol. 14 p. 74
	Steak Sukiyaki	Vol. 1 p. 42
	Steak with Madeira sauce	Vol. 8 p. 36
	Steak with tangy sauce	Vol. 8 p. 34
	Stuffed beef heart	Vol. 8 p. 105
	Stuffed cabbage rolls	Vol. 1 p. 70
	T-bone steak	Vol. 1 p. 64
	Vegetables to accompany beef	Vol. 8 p. 21
Beverages	Champagne punch	Vol. 23 p. 104
	Chocolate Madrilène	Vol. 23 p. 66
	Christmas punch	Vol. 25 p. 17
	Festive fruit punch	Vol. 23 p. 76
	Flamboyant punch	Vol. 25 p. 15
	Fruit punch	Vol. 23 p. 86
	Fruit punch (with white wine)	Vol. 25 p. 16
	Golden punch	Vol. 25 p. 15
	Hot chocolate	Vol. 23 p. 86
	Hot cider	Vol. 23 p. 56
	Hot fruit punch	Vol. 20 p. 76
	Irish coffee	Vol. 23 p. 26
	Japanese punch	Vol. 25 p. 17
	Mint tea	Vol. 23 p. 76
	Mulled wine	Vol. 25 p. 16
	Pineapple and strawberry punch	Vol. 23 p. 97
	Sangria	Vol. 25 p. 17
	Tomato cocktail	Vol. 23 p. 66
Breads	Basic methods for bread	Vol. 3 p. 30
	Bread sauce	Vol. 11 p. 28
	Garlic bread	Vol. 22 p. 28
	Hot cross buns	Vol. 9 p. 30
	Poppy seed bread	Vol. 3 p. 33
	Stuffed bread	Vol. 25 p. 20
	Sweet dough	Vol. 9 p. 28
	Whole wheat banana bread	Vol. 3 p. 34
	Whole wheat bread	Vol. 3 p. 32
Breads—Quick	Apple quick bread	Vol. 9 p. 25
	Breakfast buns	Vol. 9 p. 26
	Cranberry bread	Vol. 19 p. 100
	Pineapple and honey ring	Vol. 9 p. 24
	Quick bread dough	Vol. 9 p. 22
	Quick bread ring with nuts and green cherries	Vol. 9 p. 23

Cakes	Apple and raisin cake	Vol. 19 p. 90
	Banana cake	Vol. 3 p. 54
	Black forest cake	Vol. 25 p. 28
	Boston cream cake	Vol. 9 p. 42
	Carrot cake	Vol. 1 p. 105
	Cheesecake	Vol. 3 p. 58
	Chocolate chip cake	Vol. 23 p. 86
	Chocolate fudge cake	Vol. 3 p. 64
	Fruit cake	Vol. 3 p. 56
	German chocolate cake	Vol. 9 p. 36
	Individual cheesecakes	Vol. 22 p. 94
	Jujube cake	Vol. 25 p. 78
	Mandarin cheesecake	Vol. 9 p. 40
	Mocha cake	Vol. 25 p. 105
	Peanut butter cake	Vol. 9 p. 38
	Pineapple cake	Vol. 3 p. 52
	Queen Elizabeth cake	Vol. 3 p. 62
	Strawberry-lime chiffon cake	Vol. 23 p. 36
	Strawberry shortcake	Vol. 22 p. 92
	Successful cake making	Vol. 3 p. 48
	Tofu cheesecake	Vol. 21 p. 100
	Tomato cake	Vol. 9 p. 44
	White cake	Vol. 3 p. 55
Cassoulet	Cassoulet	Vol. 24 p. 18
Cheese	Broccoli and cheese quiche	Vol. 16 p. 86
	Camembert fritters	Vol. 16 p. 70
	Cheese and rice loaf	Vol. 16 p. 96
	Cheese and tomato flan	Vol. 16 p. 92
	Cheese ball	Vol. 16 p. 68
	Cheese cooking	Vol. 16 p. 22
	Cheese muffins	Vol. 19 p. 88
	Cheese soup	Vol. 16 p. 76
	Cheese tray	Vol. 23 p. 41
	Cheesecake	Vol. 3 p. 58
	Cheesy pudding	Vol. 20 p. 52
	Eggplant parmesan	Vol. 16 p. 72
	Fettuccine with Roquefort cheese	Vol. 12 p. 46
	Gnocchi with cheese and tomato sauce	Vol. 15 p. 84
	Individual cheesecakes	Vol. 22 p. 94
	Hot ham sandwich (Emmenthal cheese)	Vol. 14 p. 100
	Hot snack (Emmenthal cheese)	Vol. 16 p. 100
	Lasagna with four cheeses	Vol. 12 p. 38
	Macaroni and cheese	Vol. 16 p. 82
	Macaroni with cheddar cheese	Vol. 12 p. 61
	Macédoine of vegetables with cheese	Vol. 16 p. 74
	Mandarin cheesecake	Vol. 9 p. 40
	Parmesan sauce	Vol. 11 p. 22
	Parmesan white sauce	Vol. 16 p. 58
	Salmon and cheese loaf	Vol. 14 p. 88
	Swiss fondue	Vol. 16 p. 66
	Turkey and cheese casserole	Vol. 14 p. 52
Chocolate	Chocolate chip cake	Vol. 23 p. 86

Chocolate	Chocolate chip cookies	Vol.	3	p.	24
	Chocolate cream	Vol.	3	p.	82
	Chocolate fondue	Vol.	3	p.	102
	Chocolate frosting	Vol.	3	p.	69
	Chocolate fudge	Vol.	20	p.	94
	Chocolate fudge cake	Vol.	3	p.	64
	Chocolate mint mousse	Vol.	9	p.	78
	Chocolate mousse	Vol.	3	p.	101
	Chocolate muffins	Vol.	3	p.	42
	Chocolate topping	Vol.	3	p.	72
	Decorating with chocolate	Vol.	9	p.	105
	German chocolate cake	Vol.	9	p.	36
	Hot chocolate	Vol.	23	p.	86
Compotes	Apple compote	Vol.	9	p.	88
	Fruit compote	Vol.	9	p.	90
	Rhubarb compote	Vol.	9	p.	92
	Stewed peaches and plums	Vol.	23	p.	86
Cookies	Almond cookies	Vol.	18	p.	88
	Applesauce cookies	Vol.	9	p.	49
	Apricot cookies	Vol.	21	p.	98
	Oatmeal cookies	Vol.	19	p.	98
	Old-fashioned raisin cookies	Vol.	3	p.	26
	Chocolate chip cookies	Vol.	3	p.	24
	Gingerbread men	Vol.	25	p.	105
Cranberries	Cranberry and pear sauce	Vol.	2	p.	101
	Cranberry bread	Vol.	19	p.	100
	Cranberry sauce	Vol.	11	p.	30
Crepes	Banana crepes	Vol.	9	p.	98
	Apple crepes	Vol.	9	p.	99
Desserts	Almond cream	Vol.	3	p.	102
	Caramel cream	Vol.	3	p.	82
	Chantilly almond cream	Vol.	22	p.	96
	Chocolate cream	Vol.	3	p.	82
	Chocolate fondue	Vol.	23	p.	105
	Chocolate fudge	Vol.	20	p.	94
	Creamed rice with peaches	Vol.	19	p.	96
	Creamy fudge	Vol.	20	p.	102
	Crème caramel	Vol.	9	p.	84
	Crème royale	Vol.	6	p.	105
	Granola balls	Vol.	20	p.	90
	Marshmallow squares	Vol.	20	p.	86
	Mint parfait	Vol.	7	p.	105
	Pastry cream	Vol.	3	p.	100
	Rum babas	Vol.	9	p.	74
	Scones	Vol.	21	p.	94
	Strawberry cream	Vol.	3	p.	82
	Vanilla cream	Vol.	3	p.	81
Desserts with fruits	Apple and coconut Brown Betty	Vol.	9	p.	50
	Apple crisp	Vol.	3	p.	103
	Apple crumble	Vol.	9	p.	72
	Apple spice bread	Vol.	3	p.	36
	Apples with Gruyère cheese	Vol.	23	p.	27

Desserts with fruits

Apricot flan	Vol. 10	p. 105
Baked apple	Vol. 20	p. 98
Caramel and cherry ring	Vol. 9	p. 32
Caramel apples	Vol. 9	p. 48
Coconut tarts	Vol. 18	p. 92
Date squares	Vol. 3	p. 105
Fruit and pecan tart	Vol. 13	p. 105
Fruit cup with Grand Marnier	Vol. 25	p. 38
Fruit-filled pineapple	Vol. 22	p. 105
Fruit flan with pastry cream	Vol. 3	p. 98
Fruit gratin	Vol. 9	p. 57
Fruit pizza	Vol. 25	p. 50
Fruit salad	Vol. 8	p. 105
Fruit tart	Vol. 21	p. 92
Glazed pears	Vol. 21	p. 90
Hot fruit kebabs	Vol. 23	p. 87
Hzing Zen jelly	Vol. 18	p. 86
Iced melons	Vol. 23	p. 77
Molded cream with fruit sauce	Vol. 9	p. 60
Orange Charlotte	Vol. 3	p. 57
Orange crown cake	Vol. 25	p. 60
Oranges in wine	Vol. 21	p. 96
Peaches stuffed with almonds and raisins	Vol. 19	p. 92
Pears Alma	Vol. 9	p. 53
Pears in red wine	Vol. 9	p. 52
Pears with maple syrup	Vol. 9	p. 54
Pineapple flan	Vol. 9	p. 56
Pineapple fruit salad	Vol. 9	p. 58
Poached pears with raspberry coulis	Vol. 5	p. 105
Rhubarb tart	Vol. 23	p. 46
Strawberry shortcake	Vol. 3	p. 60
Strawberry shortcake (individual servings)	Vol. 22	p. 92
Strawberry trifle	Vol. 23	p. 47

Dips

Dips	Vol. 23	p. 80

Eggs

Antilles eggs	Vol. 25	p. 54
Classification of eggs	Vol. 16	p. 14
Egg and lemon soup	Vol. 24	p. 36
Egg and salmon loaf	Vol. 23	p. 34
Egg ramekins	Vol. 23	p. 61
Egg surprise	Vol. 23	p. 24
Eggs Benedict	Vol. 16	p. 42
Eggs en matelote	Vol. 16	p. 48
Eggs in ramekins	Vol. 16	p. 54
Eggs jardinière	Vol. 16	p. 46
Eggs on a muffin	Vol. 23	p. 81
Eggs poached in tomato sauce	Vol. 16	p. 45
Ham and egg terrine	Vol. 23	p. 42
Poached eggs on asparagus mousse	Vol. 23	p. 40
Scrambled egg tartlets	Vol. 16	p. 64
Scrambled eggs with rice	Vol. 16	p. 53
Scrambled eggs with smoked salmon	Vol. 16	p. 50
Shopping and storage guide for eggs	Vol. 16	p. 14

Eggs	Tomatoes stuffed with eggs	Vol. 16 p.	61
Escargots	Escargots with garlic and green onion	Vol. 6 p.	84
Fish	Bouillabaise	Vol. 5 p.	54
	Classifications of fish	Vol. 5 p.	10
	Cooking fish: methods	Vol. 5 p.	23
	Cooking fish: principles	Vol. 5 p.	24
	Defrosting fish	Vol. 5 p.	21
	Fish and fruit kebabs	Vol. 5 p.	58
	Fish and leek soup	Vol. 11 p.	78
	Fish and zucchini chowder	Vol. 5 p.	56
	Fish croquettes with shrimp sauce	Vol. 5 p.	92
	Fish stock	Vol. 11 p.	59
	Fish stock sauce	Vol. 16 p.	58
	Fisherman's stew	Vol. 19 p.	80
	Freezing fish	Vol. 5 p.	20
	Grilled fish with coriander	Vol. 24 p.	60
	Preparing fish	Vol. 5 p.	13
	Recommendations for buying fish	Vol. 5 p.	11
Fish — Bass	Steamed bass with black beans	Vol. 18 p.	56
Fish — Burbot	Burbot with lemon butter	Vol. 5 p.	83
Fish — Cod	Cod soup	Vol. 11 p.	78
	Cod steaks with vegetables	Vol. 5 p.	70
	Codfish stew	Vol. 14 p.	90
Fish — Haddock	Haddock fillets with mushroom sauce	Vol. 22 p.	68
	Haddock poached in milk	Vol. 5 p.	61
	Pilaf of haddock	Vol. 21 p.	76
	Smoked haddock	Vol. 24 p.	56
Fish — Halibut	Halibut fillets with broccoli	Vol. 5 p.	86
	Halibut steaks	Vol. 22 p.	70
	Halibut steaks in lettuce leaves	Vol. 5 p.	88
Fish — Herring	Herring Oslo style	Vol. 24 p.	88
	Marinated salt herring	Vol. 5 p.	94
Fish — Mackerel	Mackerel with leeks	Vol. 5 p.	66
	Mackerel fillets with sweet and sour sauce	Vol. 5 p.	68
Fish — Mullet	Red mullet *en papillote*	Vol. 5 p.	90
	Red mullet with lemon and chives	Vol. 24 p.	50
Fish — Norway	Norway haddock fillets on a bed of spinach	Vol. 5 p.	64
Haddock	Norway haddock with herb sauce	Vol. 5 p.	62
Fish — Perch	Perch with tomatoes	Vol. 5 p.	72
Fish — Pickerel	Pickerel fillets sautéed in butter	Vol. 5 p.	53
	Pickerel stuffed with green grapes and almonds	Vol. 5 p.	50
Fish — Salmon	Egg and salmon loaf (4 servings)	Vol. 16 p.	56
	Egg and salmon loaf (10 servings)	Vol. 23 p.	34
	Lasagna with salmon	Vol. 12 p.	40
	Salmon and cheese loaf	Vol. 14 p.	88
	Salmon loaf	Vol. 20 p.	68
	Salmon manicotti	Vol. 5 p.	34
	Salmon mousse	Vol. 22 p.	26
	Salmon omelette	Vol. 16 p.	36
	Salmon pie	Vol. 5 p.	30
	Salmon ring loaf	Vol. 5 p.	36
	Salmon steaks with duxelles	Vol. 5 p.	32

Fish — Salmon	Salmon trout with red wine	Vol. 5	p. 104
	Salmon vol-au-vent	Vol. 8	p. 100
	Salmon with Armagnac	Vol. 25	p. 34
	Salmon with dill sauce	Vol. 21	p. 80
	Scrambled eggs with smoked salmon	Vol. 16	p. 50
	Whole salmon stuffed with shrimp	Vol. 5	p. 28
Fish — Sardine	Sardine appetizer	Vol. 15	p. 30
Fish — Sea pike	Sea pike in caper sauce	Vol. 5	p. 96
Fish — Smelts	Smelts in a rosy sauce	Vol. 5	p. 82
Fish — Sole	Fillet of sole Creole style	Vol. 22	p. 74
	Fillets of sole breaded Italian style	Vol. 5	p. 46
	Fillets of sole with almonds	Vol. 5	p. 45
	Sole fillets stuffed with shrimp	Vol. 22	p. 72
	Sole mousse	Vol. 25	p. 94
	Sole roulades with a tropical sauce	Vol. 5	p. 48
	Stuffed fillets of sole	Vol. 5	p. 42
Fish — Trout	Trout *au bleu*	Vol. 5	p. 38
	Trout Mi-Chiu	Vol. 18	p. 64
	Trout with almonds	Vol. 24	p. 22
	Trout with capers	Vol. 22	p. 104
	Trout with sour cream	Vol. 5	p. 40
Fish — Tuna	Braised tuna	Vol. 24	p. 84
	Spaghetti with tuna sauce	Vol. 12	p. 28
	Tuna and noodles	Vol. 14	p. 94
	Tuna au gratin	Vol. 5	p. 80
	Tuna Florentine	Vol. 19	p. 74
	Tuna omelette	Vol. 5	p. 74
	Tuna steaks with Hollandaise sauce	Vol. 5	p. 76
	Tuna tetrazzini	Vol. 5	p. 78
Fish — Yellow perch	Yellow perch with beer	Vol. 5	p. 84
Frostings	Chocolate frosting	Vol. 3	p. 69
	Cream cheese frosting	Vol. 3	p. 69
	Japanese frosting	Vol. 3	p. 68
	Mocha frosting	Vol. 3	p. 68
Fruits — Apples	Apple and coconut Brown Betty	Vol. 9	p. 50
	Apple and raisin cake	Vol. 19	p. 90
	Apple compote	Vol. 9	p. 88
	Apple crepes	Vol. 9	p. 99
	Apple crisp	Vol. 3	p. 103
	Apple crumble	Vol. 9	p. 72
	Apple omelette	Vol. 20	p. 78
	Apple omelette flambé	Vol. 16	p. 38
	Apple pie	Vol. 17	p. 104
	Apple quick bread	Vol. 9	p. 25
	Apples with Gruyère cheese	Vol. 23	p. 27
	Applesauce	Vol. 11	p. 54
	Baked apple	Vol. 20	p. 98
	Caramel apples	Vol. 9	p. 48
	Duck with apples	Vol. 17	p. 48
	Curried apple soup	Vol. 25	p. 32
	Lamb chops with apples	Vol. 10	p. 78

Fruits — Apples	Goose with apples	Vol. 17 p.	60
Fruits — Apricots	Apricot cookies	Vol. 21 p.	98
	Apricot flan	Vol. 10 p.	105
Fruits — Avocado	Avocados with cream cheese and nuts	Vol. 15 p.	78
	Avocados with seafood	Vol. 15 p.	98
	Turkey-stuffed avocado	Vol. 14 p.	50
Fruits — Bananas	Banana cake	Vol. 3 p.	54
	Banana crepes	Vol. 9 p.	98
	Whole wheat banana bread	Vol. 3 p.	34
Fruits — Blueberry	Blueberries with yoghurt and honey	Vol. 23 p.	37
	Blueberry jam	Vol. 9 p.	95
	Blueberry pie	Vol. 24 p.	105
Fruits — Cherry	Cherry jam	Vol. 9 p.	97
	Cherry mousse	Vol. 9 p.	80
Fruits — Date	Date bran muffins	Vol. 3 p.	45
	Date squares	Vol. 23 p.	56
Fruits — Grape	Grape mousse	Vol. 9 p.	82
Fruits — Grapefruit	Grapefruit with rum	Vol. 23 p.	51
Fruits — Lemons	Lemon and pineapple pudding	Vol. 9 p.	71
	Lemon butter sauce	Vol. 18 p.	36
	Lemon meringue pie	Vol. 3 p.	94
	Lemon rice	Vol. 12 p.	82
	Lemon sauce	Vol. 11 p.	20
	Lemon topping	Vol. 3 p.	73
Fruits — Lichee	Lichee mousse	Vol. 18 p.	90
	Lichee sauce	Vol. 18 p.	70
Fruits — Oranges	Orange Charlotte	Vol. 23 p.	57
	Orange crown cake	Vol. 25 p.	60
	Orange muffins	Vol. 21 p.	86
	Oranges in wine	Vol. 21 p.	96
Fruits — Peaches	Peach halves with shrimp mousse	Vol. 22 p.	100
	Peach pie	Vol. 3 p.	91
	Peaches stuffed with almonds and raisins	Vol. 19 p.	92
	Stewed peaches and plums	Vol. 23 p.	86
Fruits — Pears	Glazed pears	Vol. 21 p.	90
	Pear and watercress soup	Vol. 23 p.	71
	Pears Alma	Vol. 9 p.	53
	Pears in red wine	Vol. 9 p.	52
	Pears with maple syrup	Vol. 9 p.	54
	Poached pears with raspberry coulis	Vol. 5 p.	105
Fruits — Pineapples	Chicken with pineapple	Vol. 18 p.	32
	Fruit-filled pineapple	Vol. 22 p.	105
	Lemon and pineapple pudding	Vol. 9 p.	71
	Pineapple and honey ring	Vol. 9 p.	24
	Pineapple and strawberry punch	Vol. 23 p.	97
	Pineapple cake	Vol. 3 p.	52
	Pineapple flan	Vol. 9 p.	56
	Pineapple fruit salad	Vol. 9 p.	58
	Pineapple salad	Vol. 23 p.	46
Fruits — Plum	Plum sauce	Vol. 18 p.	68
	Stewed peaches and plums	Vol. 23 p.	86
Fruits — Pumpkin	Pumpkin pie	Vol. 25 p.	79

Fruits — Pumpkin	Pumpkin soup	Vol. 19	p. 26
Fruits — Raisins	Old-fashioned raisin cookies	Vol. 3	p. 26
	Raisin sauce	Vol. 11	p. 54
Fruits — Raspberry	Raspberry jam	Vol. 9	p. 96
Fruits — Rhubarb	Rhubarb tart	Vol. 23	p. 46
	Rhubarb compote	Vol. 9	p. 92
Fruits — Strawberry	Strawberry cream	Vol. 3	p. 82
	Strawberry jam	Vol. 9	p. 94
	Strawberry mousse	Vol. 3	p. 102
	Strawberry pie	Vol. 3	p. 90
	Strawberry shortcake	Vol. 3	p. 60
	Strawberry shortcake (individual servings)	Vol. 22	p. 92
	Strawberry sorbet	Vol. 2	p. 105
	Strawberry trifle	Vol. 23	p. 47
Game	Aromatics and spices for game	Vol. 17	p. 45
	Cooking game: methods	Vol. 17	p. 24
	Cooking game: principles	Vol. 17	p. 22
	Defrosting game	Vol. 17	p. 20
	Hanging game	Vol. 17	p. 16
	Marinades for game	Vol. 17	p. 56
	Stuffings for game	Vol. 8	p. 57
Game — Bear	Bear stew	Vol. 17	p. 94
	Roast bear	Vol. 17	p. 92
Game — Caribou	Caribou meat loaf	Vol. 17	p. 90
	Roast caribou	Vol. 17	p. 88
Game — Deer	Deer meat stew	Vol. 17	p. 86
	Deer meat Swiss style	Vol. 17	p. 82
	Deer meat with sweet and sour sauce	Vol. 17	p. 83
	Deer steak with pepper sauce	Vol. 17	p. 84
	Leg of deer *"petit maître"*	Vol. 17	p. 80
	Roast leg of deer	Vol. 17	p. 78
Game — Duck	Duck breasts with cider	Vol. 17	p. 46
	Duck with apples	Vol. 17	p. 48
	Giblet stuffing for duck	Vol. 17	p. 57
	Roast duck stuffed with oysters	Vol. 17	p. 52
	Sauces for duck	Vol. 17	p. 58
Game — Goose	Goose stew	Vol. 17	p. 62
	Goose with apples	Vol. 17	p. 60
	Goose with cream sauce	Vol. 17	p. 64
Game — Hare	Civet of hare	Vol. 17	p. 105
	Hare casserole	Vol. 17	p. 98
	Hare hunter style	Vol. 17	p. 101
	Hare with beer	Vol. 17	p. 100
Game — Moose	Marinade for moose	Vol. 17	p. 56
	Moose meat loaf	Vol. 17	p. 72
	Moose meat with mushrooms	Vol. 17	p. 74
	Moose meatballs with cream sauce	Vol. 17	p. 76
	Moose stew	Vol. 17	p. 70
	Roast moose	Vol. 17	p. 68
Game — Partridge	Baked beans with partridge	Vol. 17	p. 36
	Partridge with cabbage	Vol. 17	p. 34
	Partridge with red wine	Vol. 17	p. 28

Game — Partridge	Partridge with sauerkraut	Vol. 17	p.	32
	Partridge with truffles	Vol. 17	p.	30
Game — Pheasant	Burgundy pheasant	Vol. 17	p.	38
	Pheasant Basque style	Vol. 17	p.	40
	Pheasant royale	Vol. 17	p.	42
Game — Quail	Quails hunter style	Vol. 17	p.	54
	Quails in wine	Vol. 23	p.	103
Garnishes	Chocolate topping	Vol. 3	p.	72
	Green pea garnish	Vol. 16	p.	60
	Lemon topping	Vol. 3	p.	73
	Mushroom garnish	Vol. 16	p.	60
	Sauces and garnishes to accompany cooked omelettes	Vol. 16	p.	58
	Spinach garnish	Vol. 16	p.	60
	Vanilla topping	Vol. 3	p.	72
Jams	Blueberry jam	Vol. 9	p.	95
	Cherry jam	Vol. 9	p.	97
	Raspberry jam	Vol. 9	p.	96
	Strawberry jam	Vol. 9	p.	94
Lamb	Aromatics and spices for veal and lamb	Vol. 10	p.	32
	Arranging cuts of lamb in the oven	Vol. 10	p.	68
	Braised lamb chops with vegetables	Vol. 10	p.	82
	Braised lamb liver	Vol. 10	p.	92
	Buying and storing lamb	Vol. 10	p.	62
	Cooking lamb	Vol. 10	p.	66
	Crown roast of lamb with apricots	Vol. 10	p.	72
	Cuts of lamb	Vol. 10	p.	60
	Defrosting lamb	Vol. 10	p.	64
	Glazed lamb shoulder	Vol. 10	p.	86
	Lamb chops English style	Vol. 22	p.	78
	Lamb chops Italian style	Vol. 10	p.	59
	Lamb chops with apples	Vol. 10	p.	78
	Lamb chops with beans	Vol. 19	p.	70
	Lamb chops with parsley	Vol. 14	p.	86
	Lamb kebabs	Vol. 10	p.	90
	Lamb meat loaf	Vol. 22	p.	82
	Lamb meatballs	Vol. 10	p.	94
	Lamb stew	Vol. 10	p.	83
	Leg of lamb glazed with cranberries	Vol. 10	p.	76
	Leg of lamb with rosemary	Vol. 10	p.	74
	Pita sandwiches with lamb meatballs	Vol. 21	p.	70
	Rack of lamb French style	Vol. 10	p.	88
	Ragoût of lamb	Vol. 10	p.	96
	Roast lamb with Madeira	Vol. 10	p.	84
	Sauces for veal and lamb	Vol. 10	p.	27
	Shank of lamb European style	Vol. 10	p.	80
	Testing lamb for doneness	Vol. 10	p.	69
Legumes — Broad beans	Broad bean soup	Vol. 19	p.	24
Legumes — Chick peas	Ratatouille with chick peas	Vol. 19	p.	42
Legumes — Lentils	Lentil and ground beef casserole	Vol. 21	p.	64

Legumes — Lentils	Lentil and tomato soup	Vol. 19 p. 32
	Lentil soup	Vol. 13 p. 100
Legumes — Navy beans	Baked beans with partridge	Vol. 17 p. 36
	Boston baked beans	Vol. 24 p. 96
	Meatballs with baked beans	Vol. 8 p. 61
Legumes — Yellow peas	Pea soup	Vol. 11 p. 96
Maple syrup	Ham with maple syrup	Vol. 4 p. 34
	Maple cream pie	Vol. 3 p. 92
	Maple ham	Vol. 23 p. 52
	Maple pie	Vol. 23 p. 56
Mousses	Ham mousse	Vol. 15 p. 92
	Salmon mousse	Vol. 22 p. 26
	Sole mousse	Vol. 25 p. 94
	Tomato mousse	Vol. 13 p. 82
Mousses for dessert	Bourbon mousse	Vol. 25 p. 70
	Cherry mousse	Vol. 9 p. 80
	Chestnut mousse	Vol. 12 p. 105
	Chocolate mint mousse	Vol. 9 p. 78
	Chocolate mousse	Vol. 3 p. 101
	Coffee mousse	Vol. 25 p. 90
	Grape mousse	Vol. 9 p. 82
	Lichee mousse	Vol. 18 p. 90
	Strawberry mousse	Vol. 3 p. 102
Muffins	Basic methods for muffins	Vol. 3 p. 40
	Cheese muffins	Vol. 19 p. 88
	Chocolate muffins	Vol. 3 p. 42
	Date and bran muffins	Vol. 23 p. 66
	Molasses bran muffins	Vol. 3 p. 44
	Orange muffins	Vol. 21 p. 86
	Wheat germ muffins	Vol. 21 p. 88
	Whole wheat honey muffins	Vol. 3 p. 43
Nuts	Avocados with cream cheese and nuts	Vol. 15 p. 78
	Coconut pie	Vol. 19 p. 94
	Coconut tarts	Vol. 18 p. 92
	Fruit and pecan tart	Vol. 13 p. 105
	Pecan pie	Vol. 3 p. 93
	Quick bread ring with nuts and cherries	Vol. 9 p. 23
Offal	Beef kidneys	Vol. 8 p. 80
	Beef liver in brown gravy	Vol. 1 p. 96
	Braised lamb liver	Vol. 10 p. 92
	Calf's brains	Vol. 10 p. 58
	Calf's liver	Vol. 10 p. 34
	Chicken liver and pork pâté	Vol. 15 p. 94
	Chicken liver and rice soup	Vol. 11 p. 86
	Chicken livers with noodles	Vol. 2 p. 68
	Liver loaf	Vol. 21 p. 45
Omelettes	Apple omelette	Vol. 20 p. 78
	Apple omelette flambé	Vol. 16 p. 38
	Beef omelette	Vol. 1 p. 74
	Chicken omelette	Vol. 2 p. 88
	Country omelette	Vol. 22 p. 86

Omelettes	Fruit omelette	Vol. 16 p. 40
	Monday omelette	Vol. 16 p. 32
	Omelette country style	Vol. 16 p. 24
	Omelette parmentier	Vol. 16 p. 62
	Omelette Provençale	Vol. 16 p. 26
	Omelette with tomato sauce	Vol. 23 p. 92
	Salmon omelette	Vol. 16 p. 36
	Sauces and garnishes to accompany cooked omelettes	Vol. 16 p. 58
	Spanish omelette	Vol. 16 p. 34
	Springtime omelette	Vol. 16 p. 30
	Tuna omelette	Vol. 5 p. 74
	Zucchini omelette	Vol. 16 p. 28
Pasta	A guide to pasta	Vol. 12 p. 10
	Beef and macaroni casserole with corn	Vol. 14 p. 32
	Cannelloni with veal and spinach	Vol. 12 p. 50
	Classic lasagna	Vol. 12 p. 34
	Cooking pasta	Vol. 12 p. 18
	Fettuccine Alfredo	Vol. 7 p. 100
	Fettuccine verde	Vol. 2 p. 92
	Fettuccine with red wine	Vol. 12 p. 45
	Fettuccine with Roquefort cheese	Vol. 12 p. 46
	Fettuccine with seafood	Vol. 6 p. 83
	Freezing and defrosting pasta	Vol. 12 p. 19
	Gnocchi with cheese and tomato sauce	Vol. 15 p. 84
	Gnocchi with cream	Vol. 12 p. 64
	Grandmother's macaroni	Vol. 8 p. 86
	Ham and macaroni casserole	Vol. 14 p. 95
	How to make fettuccine	Vol. 12 p. 44
	How to make ravioli	Vol. 12 p. 52
	Lasagna	Vol. 8 p. 88
	Lasagna with four cheeses	Vol. 12 p. 38
	Lasagna with salmon	Vol. 12 p. 40
	Leeks on a bed of noodles	Vol. 15 p. 82
	Linguine with mushrooms and cream	Vol. 12 p. 62
	Linguine with shrimps and tomatoes	Vol. 21 p. 82
	Macaroni and cheese	Vol. 16 p. 82
	Macaroni casserole	Vol. 23 p. 82
	Macaroni salad	Vol. 23 p. 30
	Macaroni stir-fry	Vol. 1 p. 92
	Macaroni with cheddar cheese	Vol. 12 p. 61
	Manicotti with pike	Vol. 12 p. 53
	Manicotti with spinach	Vol. 19 p. 84
	Pasta filled with a surprise	Vol. 12 p. 48
	Ravioli in soup	Vol. 12 p. 56
	Ravioli with scallops and fennel	Vol. 12 p. 58
	Salmon manicotti	Vol. 5 p. 34
	Spaghetti carbonara	Vol. 12 p. 24
	Spaghetti with clam sauce	Vol. 12 p. 26
	Spaghetti with meatballs and tomato sauce	Vol. 12 p. 22
	Spaghetti with tuna sauce	Vol. 12 p. 28
	Spaghettini with eggplant	Vol. 14 p. 96

Pasta	Spaghettini with garlic	Vol. 12	p. 30
	Spaghettini with seafood	Vol. 6	p. 82
	Spaghettini with vegetables	Vol. 20	p. 72
	Spinach lasagna Bolognese	Vol. 12	p. 36
	Storing pasta	Vol. 12	p. 17
	Tagliatelle with tomato sauce	Vol. 24	p. 30
	Tortellini with cream	Vol. 12	p. 54
	Tuna and noodles	Vol. 14	p. 94
	Tuna tetrazzini	Vol. 5	p. 78
	Utensils for cooking pasta	Vol. 12	p. 16
	Utensils for making pasta	Vol. 12	p. 14
Peanut butter	Peanut butter cake	Vol. 9	p. 38
Pies	Apple pie	Vol. 17	p. 104
	Blueberry pie	Vol. 24	p. 105
	Coconut pie	Vol. 19	p. 94
	Conventional pie crust	Vol. 3	p. 84
	Fruit and pecan tart	Vol. 13	p. 105
	Graham crust	Vol. 3	p. 85
	Lemon meringue pie	Vol. 3	p. 94
	Maple cream pie	Vol. 3	p. 92
	Maple pie	Vol. 23	p. 56
	Peach pie	Vol. 3	p. 91
	Pecan pie	Vol. 3	p. 93
	Salmon pie	Vol. 5	p. 30
	Strawberry pie	Vol. 3	p. 90
	Sugar pie	Vol. 3	p. 88
Pizzas	Mini-pizza	Vol. 16	p. 98
	Mini pizza Italian style	Vol. 14	p. 102
	Mini pizza Neapolitan style	Vol. 14	p. 101
	Mini pizzas	Vol. 20	p. 82
	Pizza with shrimp	Vol. 14	p. 105
	Pizzas	Vol. 20	p. 48
Pork	All purpose pork base	Vol. 4	p. 92
	Back bacon	Vol. 4	p. 84
	Buying and storing pork	Vol. 4	p. 14
	Chicken liver and pork pâté	Vol. 15	p. 94
	Chop suey with pork	Vol. 4	p. 96
	Cooking pork	Vol. 4	p. 19
	Crown roast of pork	Vol. 4	p. 104
	Cuts of pork	Vol. 4	p. 10
	Defrosting pork	Vol. 4	p. 17
	Freezing pork	Vol. 4	p. 15
	French-Canadian tourtière	Vol. 4	p. 86
	Glazed pork roast	Vol. 4	p. 24
	Golden pork chops	Vol. 4	p. 50
	Ground pork with broccoli	Vol. 18	p. 48
	Headcheese	Vol. 15	p. 96
	Homemade pork rillettes	Vol. 4	p. 82
	Hot'n spicy pork chops	Vol. 4	p. 62
	Lettuce leaves stuffed with pork	Vol. 18	p. 42
	Marinated pork tenderloin with rice	Vol. 18	p. 38
	Medallions of pork with Bordelaise sauce	Vol. 4	p. 76

Pork	Medallions of pork with fennel	Vol. 4 p. 78
	Microwaving pork	Vol. 4 p. 12
	Neapolitan pork chops	Vol. 4 p. 64
	Pigs' trotters stew	Vol. 25 p. 98
	Pigs' trotters stew (Quebec)	Vol. 24 p. 102
	Pork and onions	Vol. 14 p. 38
	Pork and potatoes with fruit sauce	Vol. 24 p. 78
	Pork chop suey	Vol. 18 p. 53
	Pork chops en papillotes	Vol. 4 p. 56
	Pork chops Normandy style	Vol. 4 p. 58
	Pork chops on macaroni	Vol. 4 p. 70
	Pork chops with a julienne twist	Vol. 4 p. 54
	Pork chops with fine herbs	Vol. 22 p. 64
	Pork chops with prunes	Vol. 22 p. 58
	Pork country style	Vol. 4 p. 80
	Pork kebabs	Vol. 4 p. 66
	Pork Kiang	Vol. 18 p. 45
	Pork meatballs	Vol. 18 p. 46
	Pork pâté	Vol. 22 p. 24
	Pork pâté (with bacon and pork liver)	Vol. 4 p. 74
	Pork spread	Vol. 23 p. 60
	Pork surprise	Vol. 4 p. 52
	Pork tenderloin Chiang Yu Wong	Vol. 18 p. 50
	Pork tenderloin Oriental style	Vol. 22 p. 62
	Pork Tsung	Vol. 18 p. 26
	Pork with fine herbs	Vol. 14 p. 42
	Pork with leeks	Vol. 14 p. 40
	Pork with red peppers	Vol. 14 p. 44
	Pork with sweet potatoes	Vol. 4 p. 83
	Pork with water chestnuts	Vol. 24 p. 66
	Rice with pork and vegetables	Vol. 12 p. 76
	Roast pork	Vol. 25 p. 46
	Roast pork stuffed with prunes	Vol. 4 p. 30
	Roast pork with potatoes	Vol. 4 p. 22
	Sauerkraut and pork	Vol. 4 p. 94
	Sausage fricassee	Vol. 4 p. 90
	Sausages and bacon	Vol. 23 p. 80
	Sausages with apple slices	Vol. 4 p. 88
	Side bacon	Vol. 4 p. 84
	Sliced pork tenderloin with fine herbs	Vol. 4 p. 72
	Spanish pork roast	Vol. 4 p. 28
	Spareribs with sweet and sour sauce	Vol. 22 p. 56
	Spices, aromatics and condiments for pork	Vol. 4 p. 20
	Sweet and sour pork chops	Vol. 4 p. 68
Pork — Ham	Broccoli and ham casserole	Vol. 13 p. 56
	Broccoli and ham rolls	Vol. 25 p. 44
	Canadian ham	Vol. 4 p. 40
	Endive and ham roll-ups	Vol. 23 p. 90
	Glazed baked ham	Vol. 4 p. 38
	Glazed ham with peaches	Vol. 11 p. 53
	Ham and egg	Vol. 20 p. 64

Pork — Ham	Ham and egg terrine	Vol. 23 p. 42
	Ham and macaroni casserole	Vol. 14 p. 95
	Ham and noodles au gratin	Vol. 4 p. 40
	Ham and watercress soup	Vol. 11 p. 84
	Ham glazed with orange	Vol. 22 p. 61
	Ham in beer	Vol. 23 p. 22
	Ham loaf	Vol. 4 p. 36
	Ham meatballs	Vol. 4 p. 46
	Ham meatballs (with pineapple rings)	Vol. 21 p. 68
	Ham mousse (with Madeira wine)	Vol. 15 p. 92
	Ham mousse (with pecans and celery)	Vol. 23 p. 102
	Ham parmentier	Vol. 4 p. 45
	Ham rolls	Vol. 15 p. 48
	Ham steak and pineapple	Vol. 4 p. 32
	Ham vol-au-vent	Vol. 4 p. 48
	Ham with maple syrup	Vol. 4 p. 34
	Hot ham sandwich	Vol. 14 p. 100
	Maple ham	Vol. 23 p. 52
	Squid stuffed with ham	Vol. 6 p. 86
Poultry	Arranging poultry parts	Vol. 2 p. 20
	Boning poultry	Vol. 2 p. 14
	Cooking poultry	Vol. 2 p. 22
	Crumb coatings (for poultry)	Vol. 2 p. 30
	Cutting a bird into equal sized pieces	Vol. 7 p. 58
	Defrosting poultry	Vol. 2 p. 30
	Flavor variations in stuffings	Vol. 2 p. 12
	Freezing poultry	Vol. 2 p. 19
	How to coat pieces of poultry	Vol. 7 p. 60
	Marinades	Vol. 2 p. 56
	Sauces	Vol. 7 p. 27
	Sauces and seasonings suitable for browning poultry	Vol. 2 p. 20
	Simple techniques to make the most of poultry	Vol. 7 p. 10
	Spices, aromatics and condiments for poultry	Vol. 2 p. 54
	Spices for poultry and for complementary sauces	Vol. 2 p. 54
	Storing poultry	Vol. 7 p. 18
	Suggested stuffings for poultry	Vol. 7 p. 40
	Vegetables to serve with poultry	Vol. 7 p. 21
Poultry — Chicken	Basic cooked chicken	Vol. 2 p. 58
	Cabbage leaves stuffed with chicken	Vol. 2 p. 90
	Chicken à la king	Vol. 2 p. 84
	Chicken and broccoli quiche	Vol. 2 p. 86
	Chicken and ham soup	Vol. 11 p. 84
	Chicken and leek pie	Vol. 23 p. 54
	Chicken and rice casserole	Vol. 18 p. 80
	Chicken and rice soup	Vol. 11 p. 91
	Chicken and rice vol-au-vents	Vol. 12 p. 96
	Chicken breasts divan	Vol. 7 p. 80
	Chicken breasts supreme (4 servings)	Vol. 2 p. 74
	Chicken breasts supreme (10 servings)	Vol. 23 p. 32
	Chicken breasts with peaches	Vol. 7 p. 82

Poultry — Chicken	Honey-glazed chicken	Vol. 18	p. 24
	Hot chicken sandwich	Vol. 7	p. 86
	How to joint a chicken	Vol. 2	p. 10
	Lemon chicken	Vol. 2	p. 64
	Lemon chicken with parsley	Vol. 2	p. 78
	Marinated chicken kebabs	Vol. 2	p. 70
	Mini chicken kebabs	Vol. 15	p. 46
	Oriental chicken	Vol. 22	p. 46
	Rice with chicken	Vol. 12	p. 94
	Roast chicken with oregano	Vol. 7	p. 74
	Saffron chicken	Vol. 2	p. 52
	Stuffed roast chicken	Vol. 7	p. 45
Poultry — Cornish Game Hen	Cornish game hens with black cherries	Vol. 7	p. 62
	Cornish game hens with sausage stuffing	Vol. 7	p. 64
	Stuffed cornish game hen	Vol. 22	p. 50
Poultry — Duck	Duck in aspic	Vol. 18	p. 34
	Duck Provençale	Vol. 7	p. 46
	Duck with olives	Vol. 7	p. 53
	Oriental duck	Vol. 7	p. 50
	Roast duck in sauce piquante	Vol. 7	p. 48
	Roast duck with orange sauce	Vol. 2	p. 44
Poultry — Goose	Goose French style	Vol. 7	p. 36
	Goose with pears in brandy	Vol. 7	p. 34
	Goose with cream sauce	Vol. 17	p. 64
Poultry — Guinea fowl	Guinea fowl with raspberries	Vol. 7	p. 104
Poultry — Quail	Quail casserole with peas	Vol. 7	p. 61
	Quails with green grapes	Vol. 2	p. 46
	Quails with onion	Vol. 7	p. 54
	Quails with white wine	Vol. 7	p. 56
Poultry — Turkey	All purpose turkey base	Vol. 14	p. 28
	Braised turkey with vegetables	Vol. 2	p. 26
	Glazes and sauces for turkey	Vol. 2	p. 23
	Holiday turkey	Vol. 25	p. 24
	Marinated turkey cutlets	Vol. 7	p. 28
	Oriental turkey	Vol. 2	p. 73
	Roast turkey	Vol. 2	p. 24
	Rolled turkey roast with herbs	Vol. 2	p. 34
	Stuffed turkey	Vol. 2	p. 104
	Tomatoes stuffed with turkey	Vol. 2	p. 41
	Turkey and bacon croquettes	Vol. 2	p. 36
	Turkey and cheese casserole	Vol. 14	p. 52
	Turkey escallops	Vol. 2	p. 28
	Turkey ring	Vol. 14	p. 46
	Turkey roulades with spinach filling	Vol. 2	p. 38
	Turkey sandwich	Vol. 7	p. 30
	Turkey stew	Vol. 2	p. 32
	Turkey-stuffed avocado	Vol. 14	p. 50
	Turkey Véronique	Vol. 14	p. 48
	Turkey with cornbread stuffing	Vol. 7	p. 22
	Turkey with paprika	Vol. 2	p. 43

Poultry — Turkey	Turkey with vegetables	Vol. 7 p. 24
Puddings	Black magic pudding	Vol. 9 p. 69
	Bread pudding	Vol. 9 p. 70
	Cheesy pudding	Vol. 20 p. 52
	Festive pudding	Vol. 23 p. 96
	Lazy pudding	Vol. 3 p. 78
	Lemon and pineapple pudding	Vol. 9 p. 71
	Plum pudding	Vol. 24 p. 54
	Rice pudding	Vol. 9 p. 66
	Rum pudding flambé	Vol. 3 p. 76
	Snowball pudding	Vol. 3 p. 79
	Tapioca pudding	Vol. 9 p. 68
Quiches	Broccoli and cheese quiche	Vol. 16 p. 86
	Cabbage quiche	Vol. 13 p. 54
	Cauliflower quiche	Vol. 15 p. 72
	Chicken and broccoli quiche	Vol. 2 p. 86
	Crab quiche	Vol. 16 p. 88
	Hamburger quiche	Vol. 8 p. 90
	Rice quiche	Vol. 12 p. 74
	Seafood quiche	Vol. 6 p. 90
	Tofu quiche	Vol. 13 p. 101
	Vegetable quiche	Vol. 23 p. 62
Rabbit	Rabbit with coconut	Vol. 24 p. 80
	Rabbit with mustard	Vol. 25 p. 56
	Rabbit with white wine	Vol. 24 p. 20
Rice	Brown rice and mushroom salad	Vol. 12 p. 101
	Cheese and rice loaf	Vol. 16 p. 96
	Chicken and rice casserole	Vol. 18 p. 80
	Chicken and rice vol-au-vents	Vol. 12 p. 96
	Chicken rice pilaf	Vol. 2 p. 59
	Clams with risotto	Vol. 6 p. 50
	Creamed rice with peaches	Vol. 19 p. 96
	Fried rice with ham and eggs	Vol. 18 p. 78
	Fried rice with shrimp	Vol. 12 p. 70
	Fried rice with soy sauce	Vol. 18 p. 74
	Indian rice	Vol. 12 p. 86
	Julienne of veal with rice	Vol. 14 p. 82
	Lemon rice	Vol. 12 p. 82
	Prawn risotto	Vol. 24 p. 28
	Rice and lobster salad	Vol. 12 p. 84
	Rice and orange stuffing	Vol. 12 p. 80
	Rice and vegetable casserole	Vol. 12 p. 88
	Rice and vegetable stuffing	Vol. 12 p. 78
	Rice pilaf	Vol. 1 p. 101
	Rice pudding	Vol. 9 p. 66
	Rice quiche	Vol. 23 p. 90
	Rice salad	Vol. 23 p. 100
	Rice with almonds	Vol. 12 p. 83
	Rice with chicken	Vol. 12 p. 94
	Rice with noodles	Vol. 20 p. 40
	Rice with tofu, Oriental style	Vol. 19 p. 46
	Rice with vegetables	Vol. 22 p. 88

Rice	Rice with pork and vegetables	Vol. 12 p. 76
	Risotto Milanese style	Vol. 12 p. 92
	Saffron rice	Vol. 12 p. 90
	Scrambled eggs with rice	Vol. 16 p. 53
	Shrimp risotto	Vol. 19 p. 76
	Steamed rice	Vol. 18 p. 101
	Tomatoes stuffed with rice	Vol. 15 p. 62
	Tsung fried rice	Vol. 18 p. 76
	Wild rice	Vol. 12 p. 72
Salads	Artichoke and mushroom salad	Vol. 13 p. 86
	Beef salad	Vol. 14 p. 76
	Brown rice and mushroom salad	Vol. 12 p. 101
	Chef's salad	Vol. 4 p. 100
	Chicken salad	Vol. 2 p. 57
	Christmas salad	Vol. 25 p. 96
	Country salad	Vol. 23 p. 60
	Crabmeat salad on croissants	Vol. 6 p. 64
	Cucumber salad	Vol. 23 p. 40
	Cucumber salad (with English cucumbers)	Vol. 10 p. 100
	Delicious aspic	Vol. 25 p. 22
	Fruit salad	Vol. 8 p. 105
	Fruit salad (fruit and canteloupe)	Vol. 23 p. 67
	Green salad	Vol. 25 p. 42
	Green salad with herbs (and Boston lettuce)	Vol. 23 p. 50
	Green salad (with Romaine lettuce)	Vol. 13 p. 104
	Hot fruit salad	Vol. 23 p. 105
	Lotus root salad	Vol. 18 p. 96
	Macaroni salad	Vol. 23 p. 30
	Mushroom and cauliflower salad	Vol. 22 p. 101
	Pineapple fruit salad	Vol. 9 p. 58
	Pineapple salad	Vol. 23 p. 46
	Rice and lobster salad	Vol. 12 p. 84
	Rice salad	Vol. 23 p. 100
	Potato salad with shrimps	Vol. 23 p. 70
	Seafood salad	Vol. 6 p. 48
	Spinach salad	Vol. 8 p. 101
	Tomato salad	Vol. 23 p. 60
	Vegetable and rice salad	Vol. 23 p. 101
	Tomato salad Italian style	Vol. 23 p. 70
Sandwiches	Hot chicken sandwich	Vol. 7 p. 86
	Hot ham sandwich	Vol. 14 p. 100
	Hot snack	Vol. 16 p. 100
	Mexican-style pita sandwich	Vol. 19 p. 72
	Pita bread snack—Greek style	Vol. 14 p. 36
	Pita sandwiches with lamb meatballs	Vol. 21 p. 70
Sauces	Anchovy sauce	Vol. 11 p. 42
	Applesauce	Vol. 11 p. 54
	(The) art of thickening sauces	Vol. 15 p. 18
	Barbecue sauce	Vol. 11 p. 48
	Béarnaise sauce	Vol. 1 p. 35
	Béchamel sauce	Vol. 11 p. 13
	Béchamel sauce with peppers	Vol. 11 p. 28

Sauces

Beef consommé sauce	Vol. 17 p.	58
Bordelaise sauce	Vol. 1 p.	34
Bread sauce	Vol. 11 p.	28
Brown sauce	Vol. 11 p.	48
Butter and dill sauce	Vol. 11 p.	18
Caper sauce	Vol. 11 p.	25
Chicken velouté sauce	Vol. 11 p.	28
Clam sauce	Vol. 11 p.	44
Cranberry and pear sauce	Vol. 2 p.	101
Cranberry sauce	Vol. 11 p.	30
Cucumber and dill sauce	Vol. 11 p.	18
Curry sauce	Vol. 11 p.	30
Deviled sauce	Vol. 11 p.	32
Espagnole sauce	Vol. 11 p.	22
Fennel sauce	Vol. 11 p.	48
Fish stock sauce	Vol. 16 p.	58
Glazes and sauces for turkey	Vol. 2 p.	23
Hollandaise Chantilly sauce	Vol. 11 p.	36
Hollandaise sauce	Vol. 11 p.	12
Horseradish sauce	Vol. 11 p.	24
Italian sauce	Vol. 1 p.	88
Italian sauce (with meat)	Vol. 11 p.	50
Italian vegetable sauce	Vol. 16 p.	59
Lemon butter sauce	Vol. 11 p.	36
Lemon sauce	Vol. 11 p.	20
Lichee sauce	Vol. 18 p.	70
Madeira sauce	Vol. 11 p.	32
Mariana sauce	Vol. 11 p.	43
Mornay sauce	Vol. 11 p.	14
Mushroom sauce	Vol. 17 p.	58
Mustard sauce	Vol. 11 p.	22
Newburg sauce	Vol. 11 p.	24
Parmesan sauce	Vol. 11 p.	22
Parmesan white sauce	Vol. 16 p.	58
Peppercorn sauce	Vol. 11 p.	48
Pesto	Vol. 11 p.	44
Plum sauce	Vol. 18 p.	68
Polonaise sauce	Vol. 11 p.	38
Provençale sauce	Vol. 11 p.	25
Raisin sauce	Vol. 11 p.	54
Red sauce	Vol. 18 p.	72
Rosy sauce	Vol. 11 p.	38
Sauce Bâtarde	Vol. 11 p.	36
Sauces and garnishes to accompany cooked omelettes	Vol. 16 p.	58
Sauces and seasonings suitable for browning poultry	Vol. 2 p.	20
Sauces for duck	Vol. 17 p.	58
Some variations on basic cold sauces (for appetizers)	Vol. 15 p.	15
Soubise sauce	Vol. 11 p.	24
Sour cream sauce	Vol. 11 p.	36

Sauces	Spinach sauce	Vol. 11 p.	43
	Sweet and sour sauce	Vol. 11 p.	18
	Sweet and sour sauce (with pineapple)	Vol. 1 p.	89
	Tartar sauce	Vol. 11 p.	18
	Teriyaki sauce	Vol. 11 p.	50
	Tomato sauce	Vol. 11 p.	42
	Vaucluse sauce	Vol. 11 p.	28
	Velouté sauce	Vol. 16 p.	58
Sauerkraut	Sauerkraut and pork	Vol. 4 p.	94
	Partridge with sauerkraut	Vol. 17 p.	32
Sorbets	Mandarin and ginger sorbet	Vol. 9 p.	62
	Strawberry sorbet	Vol. 2 p.	105
	Tomato sorbet	Vol. 6 p.	100
Soufflé	Tomato soufflé	Vol. 22 p.	30
	Pizza soufflé	Vol. 16 p.	90
Seafood	Avocados with seafood	Vol. 15 p.	98
	Buying guide (Crustaceans)	Vol. 6 p.	12
	Cleaning crustaceans	Vol. 6 p.	12
	Cooking crustaceans	Vol. 6 p.	17
	Coquilles Saint-Jacques	Vol. 6 p.	94
	Captain's plate	Vol. 6 p.	104
	Defrosting crustaceans	Vol. 6 p.	16
	Fettuccine with seafood	Vol. 6 p.	83
	Paella	Vol. 6 p.	96
	Sauces for seafood	Vol. 11 p.	16
	Seafood casserole	Vol. 6 p.	88
	Seafood chowder	Vol. 11 p.	76
	Seafood en coquille	Vol. 16 p.	80
	Seafood hors d'oeuvres	Vol. 6 p.	92
	Seafood kebabs	Vol. 6 p.	76
	Seafood quiche	Vol. 6 p.	90
	Seafood salad	Vol. 6 p.	48
	Seafood stew	Vol. 24 p.	100
	Seafood vol-au-vent	Vol. 6 p.	80
	Seafood vol-au-vents	Vol. 23 p.	44
	Spaghettini with seafood	Vol. 6 p.	82
	Storing crustaceans	Vol. 6 p.	16
Seafood — Clams	Clam sauce	Vol. 11 p.	44
	Clams au gratin	Vol. 6 p.	74
	Clams Portuguese style	Vol. 6 p.	70
	Clams with risotto	Vol. 6 p.	50
	Spaghettini with clam sauce	Vol. 12 p.	26
	Steamed clams Oriental style	Vol. 6 p.	68
	Steamed clams with garlic butter	Vol. 6 p.	66
Seafood — Crab	Chicken rolls stuffed with crab	Vol. 22 p.	53
	Crab Cantonese style	Vol. 6 p.	56
	Crab Florentine style	Vol. 6 p.	58
	Crab legs with lemon sauce	Vol. 6 p.	62
	Crab quiche	Vol. 16 p.	88
	Crab soup	Vol. 21 p.	28
	Crab vol-au-vent	Vol. 15 p.	32
	Crabmeat casserole	Vol. 6 p.	61

Seafood — Crab	Crabmeat salad on croissants	Vol. 6	p. 64
	Shelling crab	Vol. 6	p. 14
Seafood — Frogs' legs	Frogs' legs with wine and cream	Vol. 15	p. 34
	Frogs' legs Provençale	Vol. 6	p. 72
Seafood — Lobster	Cream of lobster soup	Vol. 11	p. 76
	Eggplant ragout with lobster tails	Vol. 15	p. 36
	Lobster fricassee	Vol. 23	p. 94
	Lobster meat au gratin	Vol. 6	p. 28
	Lobster Thermidor	Vol. 6	p. 24
	Lobster with mushrooms	Vol. 18	p. 54
	Rice and lobster salad	Vol. 12	p. 84
	Shelling cooked lobster	Vol. 6	p. 13
	Stuffed lobster tails	Vol. 6	p. 30
Seafood — Mollusks	Cooking mollusks	Vol. 6	p. 22
	Buying guide (mollusks)	Vol. 6	p. 18
	Storing mollusks	Vol. 6	p. 18
Seafood — Mussels	Mussels Bordelaise	Vol. 15	p. 26
	Mussels Marinière	Vol. 5	p. 101
Seafood — Oysters	Chinese vegetables with oyster sauce	Vol. 18	p. 62
	Oyster soup	Vol. 11	p. 80
	Oysters au gratin	Vol. 6	p. 54
	Oysters sautéed with mushrooms	Vol. 6	p. 78
	Roast duck stuffed with oysters	Vol. 17	p. 52
Seafood — Prawns	Prawn risotto	Vol. 24	p. 28
	Prawns in potato boats	Vol. 6	p. 46
	Prawns Italian style	Vol. 6	p. 45
	Prawns with garlic butter	Vol. 6	p. 42
Seafood — Scallops	Ravioli with scallops and fennel	Vol. 12	p. 58
	Scallops in tomato sauce	Vol. 15	p. 24
	Scallops on the half shell	Vol. 6	p. 53
	Scallops Tsao Ku	Vol. 18	p. 61
	Scallops with almonds	Vol. 14	p. 92
	Scallops with lemon and spinach	Vol. 19	p. 78
	Scallops with vegetables	Vol. 21	p. 78
Seafood — Shrimp	Couscous with chicken and shrimp	Vol. 2	p. 96
	Fried rice with shrimp	Vol. 12	p. 70
	Linguine with shrimps and tomatoes	Vol. 21	p. 82
	Pizza with shrimp	Vol. 14	p. 105
	Shelling and deveining shrimp	Vol. 6	p. 15
	Shrimp au gratin	Vol. 15	p. 22
	Shrimp bisque	Vol. 11	p. 80
	Shrimp Creole	Vol. 21	p. 74
	Shrimp in baskets	Vol. 25	p. 84
	Shrimp Kiang	Vol. 18	p. 58
	Shrimp pâté	Vol. 25	p. 102
	Shrimp risotto	Vol. 19	p. 76
	Shrimp with feta cheese in tomato sauce	Vol. 19	p. 82
	Shrimps American style	Vol. 6	p. 38
	Shrimps Chinese style	Vol. 6	p. 36
	Shrimps Creole	Vol. 6	p. 32
	Shrimps with coconut	Vol. 6	p. 40

Seafood — Shrimp	Shrimps with garlic butter	Vol. 6	p. 34
Seafood — Squid	Squid stuffed with ham	Vol. 6	p. 86
Soups	Barley and vegetable soup	Vol. 11	p. 86
	Beef soup	Vol. 21	p. 26
	Broad bean soup	Vol. 19	p. 24
	Broccoli and onion soup	Vol. 19	p. 30
	Cabbage soup	Vol. 11	p. 93
	Carrot soup	Vol. 21	p. 32
	Celery soup	Vol. 19	p. 34
	Cheese soup	Vol. 16	p. 76
	Chicken and ham soup	Vol. 11	p. 84
	Chicken and rice soup	Vol. 11	p. 91
	Chicken, ham and rice soup	Vol. 24	p. 83
	Chicken liver and rice soup	Vol. 11	p. 86
	Chicken noodle soup	Vol. 11	p. 90
	Chicken soup with snow peas	Vol. 18	p. 83
	Cod soup	Vol. 11	p. 78
	Cold soup	Vol. 11	p. 100
	Corn soup	Vol. 18	p. 82
	Crab soup	Vol. 21	p. 28
	Cream of asparagus soup	Vol. 5	p. 100
	Cream of carrot soup (beef bouillon)	Vol. 25	p. 74
	Cream of carrot soup (chicken stock)	Vol. 12	p. 100
	Cream of cauliflower soup	Vol. 11	p. 66
	Cream of celery soup	Vol. 6	p. 101
	Cream of cucumber and artichoke soup	Vol. 11	p. 72
	Cream of leek and broccoli soup	Vol. 21	p. 36
	Cream of leek and potato soup	Vol. 11	p. 72
	Cream of lobster soup	Vol. 11	p. 76
	Cream of mushroom soup	Vol. 11	p. 68
	Cream of rutabaga soup	Vol. 21	p. 30
	Cucumber and tomato soup	Vol. 21	p. 24
	Curried apple soup	Vol. 25	p. 32
	Egg and lemon soup	Vol. 24	p. 36
	Fish and leek soup	Vol. 11	p. 78
	Fisherman's soup	Vol. 19	p. 28
	Garnishes for clear soups	Vol. 11	p. 60
	Gazpacho soup	Vol. 11	p. 102
	Ham and watercress soup	Vol. 11	p. 84
	Home-style soup	Vol. 11	p. 98
	Leek soup	Vol. 1	p. 100
	Lentil and tomato soup	Vol. 19	p. 32
	Lentil soup	Vol. 11	p. 92
	Lentil soup (with red lentils and potatoes)	Vol. 13	p. 100
	Minestrone soup (beef stock)	Vol. 11	p. 96
	Minestrone soup (chicken bouillon)	Vol. 21	p. 34
	Onion soup au gratin	Vol. 11	p. 94
	Oyster soup	Vol. 11	p. 80
	Pea soup	Vol. 11	p. 96
	Pear and watercress soup	Vol. 11	p. 102
	Pumpkin soup	Vol. 19	p. 26
	Purée of pea soup	Vol. 11	p. 67

Soups	Ravioli in soup	Vol. 12 p. 56
	Seafood chowder	Vol. 11 p. 76
	Shrimp bisque	Vol. 11 p. 80
	Spicy beef soup	Vol. 24 p. 72
	Tomato and noodle soup	Vol. 11 p. 88
	Vegetable and noodle soup	Vol. 20 p. 24
	Vegetable soup	Vol. 11 p. 88
	Vegetable soup (with leeks and peppers)	Vol. 2 p. 100
	Vichyssoise	Vol. 19 p. 36
	Vichyssoise (with leeks)	Vol. 11 p. 105
	Watercress soup	Vol. 23 p. 30
	Watercress soup (with cream)	Vol. 20 p. 20
	Winter melon soup	Vol. 18 p. 96
Stocks and consommés	Chicken stock	Vol. 11 p. 58
	Compound broths	Vol. 11 p. 82
	Consommé Madrilène	Vol. 10 p. 101
	Fish stock	Vol. 11 p. 59
	Meat stock	Vol. 11 p. 58
	Vegetable stock	Vol. 11 p. 59
Stuffings	Flavor variations in stuffing	Vol. 2 p. 105
	Giblet stuffing for duck	Vol. 17 p. 57
	Rice and orange stuffing	Vol. 12 p. 80
	Rice and vegetable stuffing	Vol. 12 p. 78
	Stuffing with a fine texture	Vol. 17 p. 57
	Stuffings for game	Vol. 17 p. 57
	Suggested stuffings for poultry	Vol. 7 p. 40
Terrines	Broccoli terrine	Vol. 21 p. 42
	Ham and egg terrine	Vol. 23 p. 42
	Veal and pork terrine with cognac	Vol. 23 p. 74
Tofu	Rice with tofu, Oriental style	Vol. 19 p. 46
	Tofu cheesecake	Vol. 21 p. 100
	Tofu quiche	Vol. 13 p. 101
Tomatoes	Cheese and tomato flan	Vol. 16 p. 92
	Eggs poached in tomato sauce	Vol. 16 p. 45
	Onion and tomato casserole	Vol. 13 p. 78
	Onions with tomatoes and cream	Vol. 15 p. 80
	Stuffed tomatoes	Vol. 17 p. 104
	Tagliatelle with tomato sauce	Vol. 24 p. 30
	Omelette with tomato sauce	Vol. 23 p. 92
	Tomato and noodle soup	Vol. 11 p. 88
	Tomato cake	Vol. 9 p. 44
	Tomato ketchup	Vol. 13 p. 74
	Tomato mousse	Vol. 13 p. 82
	Tomato salad	Vol. 23 p. 60
	Tomato salad Italian style	Vol. 23 p. 70
	Tomato sauce	Vol. 11 p. 42
	Tomato sorbet	Vol. 6 p. 100
	Tomato soufflé	Vol. 22 p. 30
	Tomatoes Provençale	Vol. 13 p. 76
	Tomatoes stuffed with eggs	Vol. 16 p. 61
	Tomatoes stuffed with rice	Vol. 15 p. 62
	Tomatoes stuffed with turkey	Vol. 2 p. 41

Tomatoes	Zucchini and tomatoes in scallop shells	Vol. 19 p. 50
Tourtière	French-Canadian tourtière	Vol. 4 p. 86
	Tourtière	Vol. 25 p. 100
Veal	Aromatics and spices for veal and lamb	Vol. 10 p. 32
	Arranging cuts of veal in the oven	Vol. 10 p. 18
	Blanquette of veal	Vol. 10 p. 52
	Braised veal shank	Vol. 10 p. 36
	Buying and storing veal	Vol. 10 p. 12
	Calf's brains	Vol. 10 p. 58
	Calf's liver	Vol. 10 p. 34
	Cannelloni with veal and spinach	Vol. 12 p. 50
	Cooking veal	Vol. 10 p. 16
	Cuts of veal	Vol. 10 p. 10
	Defrosting veal	Vol. 10 p. 14
	Emincé of veal with cream sauce	Vol. 25 p. 76
	Julienne of veal with rice	Vol. 14 p. 82
	Osso bucco	Vol. 24 p. 26
	Paupiettes of veal	Vol. 10 p. 40
	Roast loin of veal	Vol. 10 p. 20
	Roast veal shoulder with cabbage	Vol. 10 p. 24
	Rolled roast of veal	Vol. 10 p. 22
	Sauces for veal and lamb	Vol. 10 p. 27
	Spinach and veal filling	Vol. 12 p. 52
	Testing veal for doneness	Vol. 10 p. 19
	Veal and pork terrine with cognac	Vol. 23 p. 74
	Veal and vegetable loaf	Vol. 21 p. 66
	Veal casserole	Vol. 10 p. 28
	Veal Cordon Bleu	Vol. 10 p. 45
	Veal escallops with mushrooms and wine	Vol. 19 p. 64
	Veal fricassee	Vol. 10 p. 54
	Veal galantine	Vol. 10 p. 50
	Veal loaf	Vol. 10 p. 56
	Veal Parmesan	Vol. 10 p. 42
	Veal ramekins	Vol. 19 p. 53
	Veal rolls	Vol. 24 p. 90
	Veal breast stuffed with spinach and ham	Vol. 10 p. 104
	Veal rump roast with apples	Vol. 10 p. 30
	Veal sauté Marengo	Vol. 10 p. 48
	Veal scallopini with cream	Vol. 12 p. 104
	Veal with stewed fruit	Vol. 10 p. 38
	Veal with vegetables	Vol. 22 p. 80
	Wiener schnitzel	Vol. 10 p. 46
	Zucchini stuffed with veal	Vol. 15 p. 38
Vegetables	Blanching vegetables	Vol. 14 p. 103
	Braised vegetables	Vol. 19 p. 40
	Buying vegetables	Vol. 13 p. 10
	Chinese vegetables with oyster sauce	Vol. 18 p. 62
	Cooking fresh vegetables	Vol. 13 p. 17
	Cooking vegetables	Vol. 22 p. 105
	Defrosting and cooking vegetables	Vol. 13 p. 16
	Festive summer vegetables	Vol. 15 p. 66
	Fiddleheads	Vol. 25 p. 49

Vegetables	Freezing vegetables	Vol. 13 p. 14
	Fried vegetables Chinese style	Vol. 13 p. 88
	Garden fresh vegetables	Vol. 13 p. 8
	Garden vegetables with vinaigrette dressing	Vol. 7 p. 101
	Glazed vegetables	Vol. 25 p. 103
	Italian vegetable sauce	Vol. 16 p. 59
	Macédoine of vegetables with cheese	Vol. 16 p. 74
	Marinated vegetables	Vol. 25 p. 59
	Mediterranean medley	Vol. 15 p. 88
	Mixed vegetables (broccoli, carrots, cauliflower)	Vol. 13 p. 50
	Mixed vegetables (broccoli, carrots, corn, cauliflower)	Vol. 15 p. 40
	Mixed vegetables (rutabaga, pepper and leek)	Vol. 25 p. 69
	Ratatouille	Vol. 13 p. 66
	Ratatouille with chick peas	Vol. 19 p. 42
	Rice and vegetable casserole	Vol. 12 p. 88
	Seasonal vegetables	Vol. 13 p. 12
	Summer vegetable combination	Vol. 13 p. 96
	Techniques for preparing fresh vegetables	Vol. 13 p. 20
	Three-vegetable garnish	Vol. 13 p. 42
	Vegetable and noodle soup	Vol. 20 p. 24
	Vegetable and shrimp platter	Vol. 23 p. 21
	Vegetable paella	Vol. 21 p. 61
	Vegetable quiche	Vol. 23 p. 62
	Vegetables and the microwave	Vol. 13 p. 26
	Vegetables au gratin (with Béchamel sauce)	Vol. 19 p. 44
	Vegetables au gratin (with Gruyère cheese)	Vol. 16 p. 94
	Vegetables au gratin (with Parmesan cheese)	Vol. 15 p. 61
	Vegetables julienne	Vol. 23 p. 80
	Vegetables Oriental style	Vol. 15 p. 90
Vegetables — Artichokes	Artichoke and mushroom salad	Vol. 13 p. 86
	Artichoke bottoms with two stuffings	Vol. 15 p. 50
	Casserole of artichokes and peas	Vol. 13 p. 83
	Stuffed artichokes	Vol. 13 p. 84
Vegetables — Asparagus	Asparagus on toast	Vol. 23 p. 30
	Asparagus with almonds	Vol. 13 p. 90
	Asparagus with Mornay or Béarnaise sauce	Vol. 15 p. 54
	Asparagus with mustard sauce	Vol. 4 p. 101
	Cream of asparagus soup	Vol. 5 p. 100
	Poached eggs on asparagus mousse	Vol. 23 p. 40
Vegetables — Bean	Green beans with tomato sauce	Vol. 13 p. 62
	Navy beans with pineapple	Vol. 21 p. 46
	Yellow beans Creole style	Vol. 13 p. 61
Vegetables — Beets	Beets julienne	Vol. 23 p. 50
	Beet ketchup	Vol. 13 p. 49
	Beets with vinegar	Vol. 13 p. 48
	Harvard beets	Vol. 19 p. 48
Vegetables — Broccoli	Broccoli and cheese casserole	Vol. 23 p. 50
	Broccoli and cheese quiche	Vol. 16 p. 86
	Broccoli and ham casserole	Vol. 13 p. 56
	Broccoli and ham rolls	Vol. 25 p. 44
	Broccoli and onion soup	Vol. 19 p. 30

Vegetables	Broccoli terrine	Vol. 21 p.	**42**
— Broccoli	Broccoli with almonds	Vol. 13 p.	**58**
	Broccoli with white wine	Vol. 21 p.	**48**
	Chicken with broccoli	Vol. 18 p.	**30**
Vegetables	Brussels sprouts with mushrooms	Vol. 13 p.	**59**
— Brussels sprouts	Brussels sprouts with sour cream	Vol. 13 p.	**60**
Vegetables	Cabbage au gratin	Vol. 15 p.	**70**
— Cabbage	Cabbage leaves stuffed with chicken	Vol. 2 p.	**90**
	Cabbage quiche	Vol. 13 p.	**54**
	Cabbage rolls	Vol. 24 p.	**48**
	Cabbage soup	Vol. 11 p.	**93**
	Orange coleslaw	Vol. 25 p.	**82**
	Stuffed cabbage rolls	Vol. 1 p.	**70**
Vegetables — Carrot	Carrot cake	Vol. 1 p.	**105**
	Carrot soup	Vol. 21 p.	**32**
	Carrots Basque	Vol. 15 p.	**56**
	Carrots with cream	Vol. 13 p.	**46**
	Cream of carrot soup	Vol. 11 p.	**64**
	Glazed carrots	Vol. 13 p.	**45**
	Vichy carrots	Vol. 25 p.	**27**
Vegetables	Cauliflower à la Polonaise	Vol. 13 p.	**60**
— Cauliflower	Cauliflower quiche	Vol. 15 p.	**72**
	Cauliflower au gratin	Vol. 1 p.	**103**
	Cream of cauliflower soup	Vol. 11 p.	**66**
Vegetables — Celery	Celery soup	Vol. 19 p.	**34**
	Cream of celery soup	Vol. 6 p.	**101**
Vegetables — Corn	Corn on the cob	Vol. 20 p.	**36**
	Corn soup	Vol. 18 p.	**82**
	Corn with chili sauce	Vol. 13 p.	**64**
Vegetables	Cream of cucumber and artichoke soup	Vol. 17 p.	**104**
— Cucumbers	Cucumber and dill sauce	Vol. 11 p.	**18**
	Cucumber and tomato soup	Vol. 21 p.	**24**
	Cucumber salad	Vol. 23 p.	**40**
	Stuffed cucumbers	Vol. 15 p.	**53**
Vegetables	Eggplant and tomato fricassee	Vol. 15 p.	**64**
— Eggplant	Eggplant parmesan	Vol. 16 p.	**72**
	Eggplant ragoût with lobster tails	Vol. 15 p.	**36**
	Eggplant with cream	Vol. 15 p.	**76**
	Moussaka	Vol. 8 p.	**62**
	Spaghettini with eggplant	Vol. 14 p.	**96**
Vegetables — Endive	Endive and ham roll-ups	Vol. 23 p.	**90**
	Endive au gratin	Vol. 16 p.	**78**
Vegetables	Green pea garnish	Vol. 16 p.	**60**
— Green pea			
Vegetables — Leek	Cream of leek and broccoli soup	Vol. 21 p.	**36**
	Cream of leek and potato soup	Vol. 11 p.	**72**
	Fish and leek soup	Vol. 11 p.	**78**
	Leek flan	Vol. 13 p.	**94**
	Leek soup	Vol. 1 p.	**100**
	Leeks on a bed of noodles	Vol. 15 p.	**82**
	Marinated leeks	Vol. 15 p.	**100**
Vegetables — Lettuce	Boston lettuce with tarragon vinegar	Vol. 23 p.	**100**

Vegetables — Lettuce	Chef's salad	Vol. 4 p. 100
Vegetables	Cream of mushroom soup	Vol. 11 p. 68
— Mushroom	Mushroom and cauliflower salad	Vol. 22 p. 101
	Mushroom garnish	Vol. 16 p. 60
	Mushroom sauce	Vol. 17 p. 58
	Mushrooms Greek style	Vol. 15 p. 101
	Stuffed mushroom caps	Vol. 23 p. 100
	Stuffed mushroom caps (with celery)	Vol. 21 p. 50
Vegetables — Onion	Onion and tomato casserole	Vol. 13 p. 78
	Onion soup au gratin	Vol. 11 p. 94
	Onions with tomatoes and cream	Vol. 15 p. 80
	Stuffed onions	Vol. 13 p. 92
Vegetables	Potato and parsnip gratin	Vol. 25 p. 101
— Parsnip		
Vegetables	Stuffed pepper canapés	Vol. 13 p. 80
— Peppers	Stuffed peppers	Vol. 1 p. 95
Vegetables	Baked potatoes	Vol. 13 p. 32
— Potato	Baked potatoes in their jackets	Vol. 20 p. 28
	Parsley potatoes	Vol. 13 p. 28
	Potato and parsnip gratin	Vol. 25 p. 101
	Potato salad with shrimps	Vol. 23 p. 70
	Potatoes stuffed with sardines	Vol. 15 p. 58
	Potatoes stuffed with sour cream and cheese	Vol. 15 p. 102
	Potatoes with a garlic stuffing	Vol. 15 p. 103
	Potatoes with onions	Vol. 13 p. 40
	Potatoes with veal stock	Vol. 13 p. 34
	Salmon-stuffed potato boats	Vol. 23 p. 91
	Scalloped potatoes	Vol. 13 p. 36
	Stuffed potatoes	Vol. 13 p. 30
	"Two-step" potatoes	Vol. 13 p. 38
Vegetables	Cream of rutabaga soup	Vol. 21 p. 30
— Rutabaga	Rutabaga and green pepper with cheese	Vol. 13 p. 53
Vegetables	Manicotti with spinach	Vol. 19 p. 84
— Spinach	Meat loaf with spinach	Vol. 1 p. 80
	Spinach garnish	Vol. 16 p. 60
	Spinach purée	Vol. 13 p. 72
	Spinach salad	Vol. 8 p. 101
	Spinach sauce	Vol. 11 p. 43
Vegetables	Watercress soup	Vol. 23 p. 30
— Watercress		
Vegetables	Fish and zucchini chowder	Vol. 5 p. 56
— Zucchini	Stuffed zucchini	Vol. 13 p. 68
	Zucchini and tomatoes in scallop shells	Vol. 19 p. 50
	Zucchini Greek style	Vol. 24 p. 34
	Zucchini Italian style	Vol. 13 p. 70
	Zucchini omelette	Vol. 16 p. 28
	Zucchini Provençale	Vol. 21 p. 53
	Zucchini stuffed with veal	Vol. 15 p. 38
	Zucchini with garlic	Vol. 25 p. 89
Whole wheat	Whole wheat banana bread	Vol. 3 p. 34
	Whole wheat bread	Vol. 3 p. 32
	Whole wheat honey muffins	Vol. 3 p. 42

Microtips
Index

A

B

Almonds (To remove the skin from)	Vol. 18 p. **91**
Almonds (To toast—in the microwave)	Vol. 4 p. **49**
Aluminum foil: an invaluable tool	Vol. 16 p. **97**
Appliances (The intelligent use of small)	Vol. 14 p. **97**
Apple (The secret for a perfectly baked)	Vol. 20 p. **98**
Apples (How to peel)	Vol. 20 p. **78**
Apricots	Vol. 19 p. **60**
Aquavit (A glass of—?)	Vol. 24 p. **88**
Aroma (The—sets the mood)	Vol. 24 p. **82**
Asparagus, broccoli and cauliflower (To cook—for cream soup)	Vol. 11 p. **86**
Aspics: for more variety	Vol. 25 p. **23**

Bacon (To separate frozen—slices)	Vol. 1 p. **49**
Bags (Cooking)	Vol. 2 p. **21**
Beans unlimited	Vol. 21 p. **12**
Beef (To defrost ground)	Vol. 8 p. **31**
Beef (To freeze ground)	Vol. 1 p. **73**
Bird (Defrosting a whole—)	Vol. 2 p. **19**
Blueberries (Choosing)	Vol. 24 p. **105**
Bouquet garni (To make a)	Vol. 4 p. **87**
Bread (Stale—for puddings)	Vol. 9 p. **59**
Bread (Success with)	Vol. 9 p. **21**
Bread (Success with quick)	Vol. 9 p. **21**
Bread (To bake—successfully)	Vol. 3 p. **37**
Bread (To defrost)	Vol. 13 p. **95**
Bread (To make—successfully)	Vol. 3 p. **31**
Bread (To reheat—rolls)	Vol. 4 p. **65**
Breadcrumbs (Homemade)	Vol. 21 p. **52**
Breadcrumbs (How to make)	Vol. 7 p. **73**
Breadcrumbs (To make your own croutons and)	Vol. 23 p. **75**
Breading (Different types of)	Vol. 5 p. **47**
Brie (What about—for fritters?)	Vol. 16 p. **71**
Broccoli (Don't waste the—stalks)	Vol. 20 p. **60**
Broccoli (How to choose)	Vol. 5 p. **87**
Broccoli (To cook)	Vol. 18 p. **38**
Butter (A simple way to make garlic)	Vol. 1 p. **55**
Butter (Don't overdo the)	Vol. 20 p. **36**
Butter (How to soften—from the refrigerator)	Vol. 4 p. **97**
Butter (Know the difference between—and margarine)	Vol. 19 p. **61**
Butter (Preparing—Meunière)	Vol. 5 p. **59**
Butter (Quick garlic)	Vol. 6 p. **93**
Butter (To clarify)	Vol. 13 p. **89**

C

Cake (Adapting traditional—recipes)	Vol. 9 p.	105
Cake (Cooking—dough successfully)	Vol. 9 p.	33
Cake (Do not overbeat—batter)	Vol. 9 p.	67
Cake (To make a—from a mix)	Vol. 3 p.	59
Cake (To turn out a—)	Vol. 9 p.	63
Cakes For even cooking	Vol. 3 p.	64
Cakes (For perfectly risen)	Vol. 3 p.	50
Cakes (To make—successfully)	Vol. 3 p.	48
Cakes (To test if—are cooked)	Vol. 1 p.	105
Calf's liver (Storing)	Vol. 10 p.	17
Cannelloni (To cook—and lasagna quickly)	Vol. 12 p.	60
Carrots (How to cut—into rounds)	Vol. 20 p.	32
Cauliflower (To cook asparagus, broccoli and—for cream soup)	Vol. 11 p.	86
Cheese (Pasta and)	Vol. 12 p.	31
Cheese (Cleaning the—grater)	Vol. 15 p.	59
Cheese (How to serve)	Vol. 16 p.	23
Cheese (Keeping grated—on hand)	Vol. 12 p.	60
Cheese (To grate—more easily)	Vol. 15 p.	22
Cheese (Use—instead of butter and salt)	Vol. 12 p.	27
Cheese (Which—to choose?)	Vol. 12 p.	38
Cheeses (Using a variety of)	Vol. 12 p.	60
Cheesecake (A delicious crust for)	Vol. 16 p.	71
Chicken (Defrosting boneless)	Vol. 7 p.	15
Chicken (Defrosting—breasts)	Vol. 2 p.	18
Chicken (Defrosting—legs)	Vol. 7 p.	95
Chicken (Defrosting—pieces)	Vol. 7 p.	17
Chicken (For crispy)	Vol. 7 p.	87
Chicken (Roasting a whole)	Vol. 7 p.	77
Chicken (The proper way to defrost)	Vol. 11 p.	30
Chicken (To bake tender)	Vol. 2 p.	22
Chicken (To cook a—successfully)	Vol. 2 p.	22
Chicken (To defrost—breasts)	Vol. 23 p.	85
Chicken (To tenderize)	Vol. 7 p.	87
Chili powder and chili peppers	Vol. 19 p.	73
Chocolate (Grating—easily)	Vol. 9 p.	89
Chocolate (To coat with)	Vol. 3 p.	25
Chocolate (To melt)	Vol. 9 p.	20
Coconut: the secret of really great chilled soup	Vol. 11 p.	102
Coconut (To break open a)	Vol. 18 p.	91
Coffee (To reheat)	Vol. 6 p.	87
Compote (Don't let the—become a purée)	Vol. 9 p.	91
Compote (For a tastier)	Vol. 25 p.	33
(To) cook a chicken successfully	Vol. 2 p.	22
(To) cook broccoli	Vol. 18 p.	38
Cooked quiche (How to tell if a quiche is cooked)	Vol. 16 p.	87
Cookies (How to make your—golden)	Vol. 3 p.	23
Cookies (To make—successfully)	Vol. 3 p.	27
Containers (Filling—with narrow necks)	Vol. 14 p.	49
Cooking bags (How to use)	Vol. 7 p.	26
Cooking *of cakes* (For even—)	Vol. 3 p.	64
Cooking (Defrosting and—combined)	Vol. 1 p.	22
Cooking duck	Vol. 2 p.	45
Cooking fruits together	Vol. 9 p.	93
Cooking *of meat* (For even)	Vol. 17 p.	38
Cooking mussels	Vol. 15 p.	26
Cooking odors (To rid the oven of)	Vol. 4 p.	29
Cooking *vegetables* (For uniform)	Vol. 13 p.	57
Corn A crunchy Mexican treat	Vol. 19 p.	67
Corn (What do you know about—?)	Vol. 20 p.	39
Crab legs (Removing the meat from)	Vol. 6 p.	63
Crabmeat (Some simple and inexpensive ways to enjoy)	Vol. 6 p.	60
Croquettes (Making—or rice pudding)	Vol. 12 p.	81
Croutons (To make your own—and breadcrumbs)	Vol. 23 p.	75

D

(To) defrost chicken breasts — Vol. 23 p. 85
(To) defrost fruit in plastic bags — Vol. 14 p. 77
(To) defrost fruit in cartons — Vol. 14 p. 45
Defrost (The proper way to—chicken) — Vol. 11 p. 30
Defrost (To freeze and—cheese) — Vol. 16 p. 105
Defrosting a whole bird — Vol. 2 p. 19
Defrosting and cooking combined — Vol. 1 p. 22
Defrosting and reheating combined — Vol. 17 p. 65
Defrosting chicken legs — Vol. 7 p. 95
Defrosting chicken pieces — Vol. 7 p. 17
Defrosting *of meat* (For even) — Vol. 17 p. 21
Defrosting (For perfect) — Vol. 22 p. 17
Defrosting (Proper freezing for easier) — Vol. 14 p. 105

Deglazing (A special—technique) — Vol. 11 p. 32
Desserts (Make your—more nutritious) — Vol. 21 p. 79
Desserts (Low-calorie) — Vol. 19 p. 95
Desserts (Low-cost) — Vol. 19 p. 95
Dessert (To improve a too sweet) — Vol. 9 p. 61
Dessert (To unmold a frozen) — Vol. 9 p. 39
Diet (For people on a) — Vol. 16 p. 65
Dips (Instant) — Vol. 16 p. 87
Dish (Preheating browning) — Vol. 1 p. 37
Dish (Using an earthenware casserole) — Vol. 10 p. 19
Dishes (Ring) — Vol. 5 p. 37
Drumsticks (Freezing breaded) — Vol. 7 p. 73
Duck (Defrosting pieces of) — Vol. 2 p. 45
Duck (Cooking) — Vol. 2 p. 45

E

Egg (Beating—whites) — Vol. 16 p. 26
Egg (To maximize the volume of—whites) — Vol. 9 p. 67
Egg yolks (Preventing—from getting hard) — Vol. 16 p. 15
Eggs at room temperature — Vol. 16 p. 14
Eggs (Beware of cooking—à la coque) — Vol. 16 p. 15
Eggs (Cooking times for poached) — Vol. 16 p. 77
Eggs (Don't let your—bomb!) — Vol. 20 p. 44
Eggs (Hard-boiled—without dark rings) — Vol. 14 p. 45

Eggs (How to test—for freshness) — Vol. 23 p. 35
Eggs in ramekins—without ramekins — Vol. 16 p. 54
Eggs, please! — Vol. 20 p. 47
Eggs (Scrambled) — Vol. 8 p. 91
Eggs, scrambled Caught unaware? Never! — Vol. 16 p. 47
Eggs (Storing) — Vol. 23 p. 25
Eggs Sunny side up — Vol. 20 p. 64
Endive (To keep—from discoloring during cooking) — Vol. 13 p. 91
Entertaining (For successful) — Vol. 25 p. 12

F

Filling containers with narrow necks — Vol. 14 p. 49
Fine herbs (To dry) — Vol. 10 p. 73
Fish (Cook—carefully to retain its delicate flavor) — Vol. 5 p. 23
Fish (Do not overcook) — Vol. 5 p. 65
Fish (How to stuff a whole) — Vol. 5 p. 13
Fish (Storing fresh) — Vol. 5 p. 31
Fish (To cook—successfully) — Vol. 11 p. 20
Fish (To defrost and cook—sticks) — Vol. 5 p. 71
Fish (To defrost—steaks) — Vol. 5 p. 89
Fish (To prevent—from cooking in its own juices) — Vol. 5 p. 63
Fish (To sear) — Vol. 5 p. 41
Fish stock (What makes a really good—?) — Vol. 11 p. 78
Flans (How to cook—evenly) — Vol. 16 p. 93
Fondue (To keep a—very hot) — Vol. 16 p. 87
Food (Restoring freshness to) — Vol. 5 p. 95
(To) freeze and defrost cheese — Vol. 16 p. 105
(To) freeze ground beef — Vol. 1 p. 73
(To) freeze meat loaf — Vol. 1 p. 85
Freezing (A practical suggestion for) — Vol. 5 p. 65
Freezing and defrosting mollusks — Vol. 6 p. 19
Freezing for easier defrosting — Vol. 22 p. 83
Freezing irregularly shaped cuts — Vol. 1 p. 15
Freezing pasta — Vol. 14 p. 38
Freezing (Preparing meat for) — Vol. 8 p. 57
Freezing (Some tips on) — Vol. 22 p. 29
Frozen foods (Cooking) — Vol. 22 p. 59
Fruit (To defrost—in cartons) — Vol. 14 p. 45
Fruit (To defrost—in plastic bags) — Vol. 14 p. 77
Fruit (Cooking—together) — Vol. 9 p. 93
Fruits (Embellishing—and vegetables) — Vol. 15 p. 63
Fruits (Protecting the flavor of certain) — Vol. 9 p. 55

G

Game For even cooking — Vol. 17 p. 38
Game (Getting the best flavor from) — Vol. 17 p. 69
Garlic (A—substitute) — Vol. 19 p. 35
Garlic (To peel and crush—with a knife) — Vol. 23 p. 65
Garlic butter (A simple way to make) — Vol. 1 p. 55
Garlic cloves (To peel—more easily) — Vol. 1 p. 59
Glaze (An easy—for roast veal) — Vol. 10 p. 57
(To) glaze (To cook and—a ham steak) — Vol. 23 p. 53
Glazes (Sweet) for pork — Vol. 4 p. 38
Green pepper (Leftover) — Vol. 8 p. 79
Grocery lists (Fool proof) — Vol. 14 p. 73
Ground meat (To remove the fat from) — Vol. 10 p. 73

H-I

Haddock (To defrost—fillets) — Vol. 5 p. 97
Ham meatballs To make a meal for one — Vol. 21 p. 69
Ham (To cook and glaze—steak) — Vol. 23 p. 53
Health Are you a good cook? — Vol. 20 p. 86
Health Professional approach (The) — Vol. 19 p. 85
Herbs (Fresh homegrown) — Vol. 15 p. 95
Herbs (To dry fresh) — Vol. 19 p. 59
Herbs (To make the most of dried) — Vol. 10 p. 91
Ham steak (Cooking a) — Vol. 4 p. 63
Ham steak (To glaze a) — Vol. 4 p. 44

Iron (To get enough) — Vol. 21 p. 59

K-L M

Knives (Sharpening—: a delicate
but indispensable task) ... Vol. 5 p. 15

Lasagna (To cook cannelloni
and—quickly) ... Vol. 12 p. 60
Leftover (Freezing and
defrosting—rice) ... Vol. 12 p. 77
Leftover (Ideas for—seafood) ... Vol. 6 p. 52
Leftover (Use—rice in soups) ... Vol. 12 p. 73
Leftover sauce for
making . . . sauces! ... Vol. 18 p. 69
Leftovers (For delicious *seafood*) ... Vol. 6 p. 38
Leftovers (To reheat) ... Vol. 4 p. 81
Lettuce (Cutting—in ribbons) ... Vol. 13 p. 104
Lemon and orange zest (To store) ... Vol. 10 p. 91
Lamb (Choosing) ... Vol. 10 p. 71
Lamb (For tender) ... Vol. 10 p. 77
Lamb (To marinate veal
or—effectively) ... Vol. 10 p. 105
Lamb (Two traditional sauces for) ... Vol. 10 p. 89
Leftovers (A different way
to serve—) ... Vol. 1 p. 55
Leftovers (To reheat) ... Vol. 4 p. 81
Lentils ... Vol. 19 p. 18
Legumes (Dry) ... Vol. 21 p. 37
Legumes (The use of dry—in different
cooking traditions) ... Vol. 21 p. 19
Leeks (How to choose) ... Vol. 22 p. 89
Leeks (How to clean) ... Vol. 23 p. 55
Lettuce (Cutting—in ribbons) ... Vol. 13 p. 104
Lobster (Killing) ... Vol. 6 p. 23
Lobster (Removing the meat from a) ... Vol. 23 p. 95

Marinade (Don't throw the—away!) ... Vol. 20 p. 59
Marinating less tender cuts ... Vol. 1 p. 25
(To) marinate veal or lamb effectively ... Vol. 10 p. 105
Meal (For a quick) ... Vol. 13 p. 52
(To) measure fat ingredients easily ... Vol. 9 p. 37
(To) measure your liquid
ingredients accurately ... Vol. 20 p. 72
Meat needs company ... Vol. 21 p. 59
Meat (Preparing for freezing) ... Vol. 8 p. 57
Meat (Searing) ... Vol. 8 p. 17
Meat (To flour) ... Vol. 8 p. 59
Meat (To prevent ground—from
sticking to your fingers) ... Vol. 10 p. 97
Meat loaf (To freeze) ... Vol. 1 p. 85
Meat loaf (To test if—is done) ... Vol. 4 p. 97
Meatballs (Arranging for cooking) ... Vol. 8 p. 93
Meatballs (For even defrosting and
cooking of cubes and) ... Vol. 8 p. 41
Meatballs, shaping Don't get stuck! ... Vol. 20 p. 90
Microwaves and liquids ... Vol. 5 p. 24
Microwaves and metal do not mix! ... Vol. 5 p. 25
Milk (Chocolate—with a difference) ... Vol. 20 p. 97
Milk (How to made a glass
of—special) ... Vol. 20 p. 82
Mollusks (Freezing and defrosting) ... Vol. 6 p. 19
Mollusks (Serving) ... Vol. 6 p. 22
Mousse (Making a great) ... Vol. 25 p. 91
Mousse (Making the best) ... Vol. 9 p. 81
Muffins (Making healthy) ... Vol. 19 p. 91
Mushrooms ... Vol. 1 p. 43
Mushrooms (To clean) ... Vol. 11 p. 91
Mussels (Removing filaments from) ... Vol. 6 p. 21
Mussels (Cooking) ... Vol. 15 p. 26

N-O   P-Q

Nuts (To shell)   Vol. 3 p. 14

Omelette (For a succulent fruit)   Vol. 16 p. 47
Omelette (How to prepare a perfect)   Vol. 16 p. 38
Onions (Baked—? Why not?)   Vol. 15 p. 60
Onions (Cleaning your knife
  after slicing)   Vol. 15 p. 60
Onions (Cooking with)   Vol. 15 p. 60
Onions (Keeping your friends
  while enjoying)   Vol. 15 p. 60
Opening jars easily   Vol. 15 p. 97
Oranges (Preserving the Vitamin C in)   Vol. 19 p. 68
Overcooking (Avoid)   Vol. 15 p. 83
Oysters (To open)   Vol. 18 p. 63

Pan (An ideal utensil: The tube)   Vol. 16 p. 77
Parsley (Another way to use fresh)   Vol. 15 p. 29
Pasta and cheese   Vol. 12 p. 31
Pasta (Color your—!)   Vol. 19 p. 52
Pasta (Cooking and reheating)   Vol. 11 p. 44
Pasta: different flavors but
  similar nutrients   Vol. 21 p. 83
Pasta (Freezing)   Vol. 14 p. 38
Pasta with a splendid yellow color   Vol. 12 p. 57
Pastry shells (For perfect—in
  the microwave oven)   Vol. 2 p. 12
Patty shell (The versatile)   Vol. 23 p. 45
Pears (To prevent—from
  turning brown)   Vol. 21 p. 91
Periwinkles, whelks, or snails
  (To extract—from their shells)   Vol. 6 p. 71
Pie crust (To prevent a—from
  going soggy)   Vol. 3 p. 95
Pizza (A—without dough)   Vol. 16 p. 91
Plum pudding: a quintessential
  British tradition   Vol. 24 p. 55
Pork (To test if—is done)   Vol. 4 p. 95
Pork chops (Another way to prepare)   Vol. 4 p. 54
Potatoes (For perfectly cooked)   Vol. 13 p. 38
Potatoes (How do you know when
  the—are done?)   Vol. 20 p. 28
Poultry (Chilling—promptly)   Vol. 7 p. 19
Poultry (Cooking individual—pieces)   Vol. 7 p. 19
Poultry For crisp skin   Vol. 2 p. 79
Poultry (Freezing—for future use)   Vol. 7 p. 19
Poultry (How to cook—with less fat)   Vol. 2 p. 22
Poultry (How to roast—successfully)   Vol. 7 p. 31
Poultry (How to stuff)   Vol. 7 p. 15
Poultry (Leftover)   Vol. 7 p. 19
Poultry (Preparing—for cooking)   Vol. 2 p. 14
Poultry (Testing for doneness)   Vol. 11 p. 68
Poultry (To avoid soft, moist skin
  when cooking)   Vol. 2 p. 63
Probe (How to cook using
  the temperature)   Vol. 1 p. 44
Pudding (To make from a mix)   Vol. 3 p. 77
Pudding (Stale bread for)   Vol. 9 p. 59

Quantities (Making smaller   Vol. 13 p. 44
Quiche (How to tell if a—is cooked)   Vol. 16 p. 87

R

(To) reduce a recipe | Vol. 2 p. 29
Reheat foods (To—that cannot be stirred) | Vol. 13 p. 97
Reheat (To—bread rolls) | Vol. 4 p. 65
Reheating | Vol. 2 p. 27
Reheating (Cooking and—pasta) | Vol. 11 p. 44
Reheating (Defrosting and —combined) | Vol. 17 p. 65
Reheating individual portions | Vol. 22 p. 37
Rice as fiber | Vol. 19 p. 47
Rice (Cooking—in the microwave oven) | Vol. 18 p. 59
Rice (Cooking long grain—in the microwave oven) | Vol. 5 p. 105
Rice (Cooking times for) | Vol. 12 p. 69
Rice (For fluffy) | Vol. 12 p. 79
Rice (Freezing and defrosting leftover) | Vol. 12 p. 77
Rice (How to cook—so it's really good) | Vol. 20 p. 40
Rice (Instant—: what is it?) | Vol. 18 p. 81
Rice (Quick—with tomato juice) | Vol. 12 p. 93
Rice or vegetables (To cook—in a dish without a cover) | Vol. 18 p. 54
Rice pudding (Making croquettes or) | Vol. 12 p. 81
Rice (Saffron) | Vol. 12 p. 105
Rice: swell stuff! | Vol. 20 p. 43
Rice (Use leftover—in soups) | Vol. 12 p. 73
Rice (Which—should you choose?) | Vol. 18 p. 60
Rice: white, brown or semi-cooked | Vol. 19 p. 63
Rice with orange juice | Vol. 12 p. 93
Rice with vegetable juice | Vol. 12 p. 93
Risotto (Making) | Vol. 12 p. 91
Roux (White—: a base for white sauces) | Vol. 11 p. 70

S

Safety Don't cut yourself! | Vol. 20 p. 35
Safety Fingers (Mind your—!) | Vol. 20 p. 24
Safety (Wear your oven mitts) | Vol. 20 p. 94
Safety Watch out for the steam!) | Vol. 20 p. 102
Salt (Watch out for hidden) | Vol. 19 p. 61
Salt (With regard to) | Vol. 7 p. 97
Sauce (Aioli—A delicious—from Provence) | Vol. 6 p. 44
Sauce (Choose the right) | Vol. 5 p. 49
Sauce (For a creamy) | Vol. 15 p. 24
Sauce (For spaghetti—that is less fattening) | Vol. 10 p. 52
Sauce (To make great barbecue) | Vol. 7 p. 54
Sauces (About:—classic combinations) | Vol. 15 p. 77
Sauces (Add a little zest to your) | Vol. 11 p. 54
Sauces: adding flair to game | Vol. 17 p. 55
Sauces (Hints for successful) | Vol. 11 p. 50
Sauces (Leftover—for making . . . sauces!) | Vol. 18 p. 69
Sauces (To rescue) | Vol. 11 p. 38
Sauces (Two traditional—for lamb) | Vol. 10 p. 89
Sauerkraut (What is—?) | Vol. 24 p. 47
Scallops (How to choose) | Vol. 21 p. 79
Scallops (Buying) | Vol. 6 p. 19
Seafood Flavors (A delicious mix of) | Vol. 6 p. 79
Seafood (Ideas for leftover) | Vol. 6 p. 52
Seafood (Wines to serve with) | Vol. 6 p. 105
Shrimp (Add variety to—dishes) | Vol. 6 p. 20
Shrimp (Butterflying) | Vol. 6 p. 12
Shrimp (Defrosting) | Vol. 6 p. 21
Shrimp (Shelling fresh) | Vol. 6 p. 35
Shrimps: (An easy way to cook) | Vol. 11 p. 76
Smörgasbord (The) | Vol. 24 p. 89
Snacks (Healthy) | Vol. 19 p. 61
Snails (To extract periwinkles, whelks, or—from their shells) | Vol. 6 p. 71
Soups: conventional cooking or microwave method? | Vol. 11 p. 72
Soups (Homemade—in a hurry) | Vol. 11 p. 88
Spinach (To wash) | Vol. 11 p. 94
Squash (Enjoy stuffed—throughout the year) | Vol. 21 p. 31
Stains (Removing food) | Vol. 17 p. 77
Steaks (To defrost) | Vol. 8 p. 49
Stocks and their evolution | Vol. 11 p. 64
(To) stuff (How—a whole fish) | Vol. 5 p. 13
(To) stuff (How—poultry) | Vol. 7 p. 15
Substitutes | Vol. 3 p. 73
Sugar (Cooking with) | Vol. 9 p. 67
Sugar (To soften brown) | Vol. 3 p. 21
Sugar (Watch out for) | Vol. 9 p. 51

T-U

Technology to the rescue — Vol. 16 p. 65
Thermometer (The meat) — Vol. 22 p. 60
Thickening agents — Vol. 11 p. 15
Tofu: an excellent source of protein — Vol. 19 p. 61
Tomatoes (About) — Vol. 21 p. 41
Tomatoes (To peel) — Vol. 8 p. 71
Turkey (To prepare a—for cooking) — Vol. 2 p. 30
TV dinner in just a few seconds (For a) — Vol. 1 p. 18
Twist ties (Instead of) — Vol. 23 p. 23

(To) unmold a frozen dessert — Vol. 3 p. 105
Utensils Cutting and chopping—Oriental style — Vol. 24 p. 71

V

Veal (An easy glaze for roast) — Vol. 10 p. 57
Veal (Barding a roast of) — Vol. 10 p. 49
Veal Shoulder Roast—A Good Choice — Vol. 10 p. 57
Veal (To flatten—escallops) — Vol. 10 p. 51
Veal or lamb (To marinate—effectively) — Vol. 10 p. 105
Vichyssoise — Vol. 11 p. 105
Vegetable side dishes — Vol. 17 p. 61
Vegetables (Blanching—successfully) — Vol. 14 p. 31
Vegetables (Choosing—for blanching) — Vol. 14 p. 89
Vegetables (Cooking) — Vol. 1 p. 27
Vegetables (Cooking frozen—at 100% power) — Vol. 25 p. 88
Vegetables (Cooking times for blanched) — Vol. 14 p. 89
Vegetables (Determining cooking time for a mixture of) — Vol. 13 p. 29
Vegetables (Embellishing fruits and) — Vol. 15 p. 63
Vegetables For best results — Vol. 13 p. 29
Vegetables (For perfectly cooked) — Vol. 13 p. 25
Vegetables For uniform cooking — Vol. 13 p. 57
Vegetables in New England stew

Variations welcome! — Vol. 24 p. 95
Vegetables A quick side dish — Vol. 14 p. 87
Vegetables (Keeping—fresh and flavorful) — Vol. 15 p. 79
Vegetables (Knowing when—have lost their nutrients) — Vol. 19 p. 45
Vegetables (Practical suggestions for cooking) — Vol. 5 p. 57
Vegetables Frozen foods (Preparing—quickly) — Vol. 13 p. 65
Vegetables (Preserving vitamins in) — Vol. 21 p. 16
Vegetables (Rapid blanching of) — Vol. 22 p. 82
Vegetables (To cook—evenly) — Vol. 2 p. 33
Vegetables (To cook rice or—in a dish without a cover) — Vol. 18 p. 54
Vegetables (To defrost half a package of) — Vol. 10 p. 67
Vegetables (To defrost small servings of) — Vol. 13 p. 79
Vegetables (To speed up the cooking times for firm) — Vol. 14 p. 47
Vegetables (Using frozen) — Vol. 25 p. 88
Venison (For successful—roasts) — Vol. 17 p. 25
Vitamin C (Preserving—in oranges) — Vol. 19 p. 68

W-Z

Water (Drink plenty of) — Vol. 19 p. 60
Watercress (The easy way to wash) — Vol. 20 p. 20
Water (Mineral) — Vol. 19 p. 60
Whelks (To extract periwinkles,—, or snails from their shells) — Vol. 6 p. 71
Wines to accompany game — Vol. 17 p. 41
Wines to accompany your meals — Vol. 22 p. 107
Wines to serve with seafood — Vol. 6 p. 105

Zucchini (Other fillings for) — Vol. 15 p. 38